D1098623

ALLEN, Paul
A pocket guide to Alan Ayckbourn's plays

Please return/renew this item by the last date shown.
Fines will be payable if items are returned late.
Thank you for using Castle Learning Resource Centre.

The Sheffield College – Castle Centre
Tel. 0114 260 2134

by Alan Ayckbourn
THE CRAFTY ART OF PLAYMAKING

by Paul Allen
ALAN AYCKBOURN: GRINNING AT THE EDGE

other books in the Pocket Guide series
A POCKET GUIDE TO SHAKESPEARE'S PLAYS
Kenneth McLeish and Stephen Unwin

A POCKET GUIDE TO TWENTIETH-CENTURY DRAMA
Stephen Unwin with Carole Woddis

A POCKET GUIDE TO IBSEN, CHEKHOV AND STRINDBERG
Stephen Unwin and Michael Pennington

A POCKET GUIDE TO OPERA
Rupert Christiansen

A POCKET GUIDE TO
Alan Ayckbourn's Plays

Paul Allen

faber and faber

First published in 2004
by Faber and Faber Limited
3 Queen Square London WC1N 3AU
Published in the United States by Faber and Faber Inc.
an affiliate of Farrar, Straus and Giroux LLC, New York

Typeset by Faber and Faber Limited
Printed in England by Bookmarque Ltd, Croydon

The right of Paul Allen to be identified as author of this work has
been asserted in accordance with Section 77 of the Copyright,
Designs and Patents Act 1988

A CIP record for this book
is available from the British Library

ISBN 0-571-21492-4

10 9 8 7 6 5 4 3 2 1

Contents

Introduction

Who and what is Alan Ayckbourn? Statistics tell some of the story. He has written over sixty plays (whatever it was at the last count is *always* out of date), of which some thirty-five have been seen in London. He set a record by having five running simultaneously in the West End, and another by having four running simultaneously on Broadway. His work has been translated into forty languages and seen round the world. So he is popular, possibly the most popular any playwright has ever been in his own lifetime. He is funny. There are numerous accounts of theatre tannoy systems being put out of action by the sheer volume of laughter known as the 'Ayckbourn roar'. And he is admired by the critics of six continents: he has been described as the modern Molière, an English Chekhov, even a seaside Ibsen.

But neither statistics nor reviews convey the unique quality of a writer who has tapped into the collective psyche of a generation while remaining a one-off.

In a sense, he has been lucky. He made personal relationships his special subject at precisely the time the institutions of marriage and the nuclear family began to fall into terrible disarray – while remaining the aspiration of the bulk of the population. With no obvious solutions in sight to the problems of how people are to live together, Ayckbourn's plays are broadly and blissfully relevant to us all. Ideology and party politics hardly ever feature in Ayckbourn's plays, but if 'the personal is political' he is a profoundly political writer, our most authentic chronicler of a social revolution.

No other writer so regularly generates a roar of laughter followed by the horrified realization of just what we are laughing at. Ayckbourn has ushered in another revolution by going further than anyone else in pointing out that things that are funny are also the stuff of tragedy.

He has an unmatched record in experimenting with form

in almost every play he writes, but his inventive adroitness at characterization and story-telling is such that playgoers rarely feel experimented upon. This last quality – the ability to break new ground while feeling utterly familiar – perhaps explains why Ayckbourn's individual plays have generated huge critical enthusiasm but his name rarely crops up in analyses of theatrical trends: he is simply not hard going enough to be treated as revolutionary.

We should also add that he achieves all this as a man who is far from politically correct but who writes with an unparalleled and instinctive understanding of the range of women's experience and psychology. His heroines are never idealized into sainthood; they are far more interesting.

Alan Ayckbourn was born in Hampstead, London, on 12 April 1939, and few playwrights can have been more fully fashioned by birth and upbringing. His father, Horace Ayckbourn, was a violinist, deputy leader of the London Symphony Orchestra, and his mother, known variously as Rene M. Worley and Mary James, was a writer of novels and short stories. By the time he was six, his parents had separated and he was living with his mother in a farm cottage in Sussex. While she typed stories for women's magazines on the kitchen table, he hammered away alongside her at the small portable she had bought to keep him quiet. He learned that writing was a way you could make a living. He also learned to perceive the adult world chiefly through his mother's experience.

The idyll was short-lived, however. When his mother, anxious about money and discipline, sent him to a nearby boarding school, he underwent a crash course in the way intimate affection can suddenly be withdrawn. Shortly afterwards, she wrote to him there to say she was marrying her bank manager, Cecil Pye.

The marriage was profoundly unhappy – the Bohemian 'Lolly' as she was commonly known and respectable Cecil were blazingly incompatible – but it lasted for nine years, starting when Ayckbourn was eight years old. The impressionable child was given a ringside view of spectacular rows and silent misery, but also of scenes of terrible comedy.

The young Ayckbourn filled much of his relatively solitary childhood with the cinema, and many of his later impulses to push at the boundaries of what stories theatre can tell have been inspired by films. He also invented complex imaginative games and enjoyed music, cricket and conjuring. At first, he shone academically. And he wrote plays, adapting one of Anthony Buckeridge's comic novels of prep-school life for his own prep school. Later, at Haileybury, he acted in school Shakespearean productions and joyfully discovered Whitehall farce. He left school at seventeen with two A levels (English and History) and the ambition to become an actor. His school connections led to an expenses-only job with the great actor–manager Sir Donald Wolfit.

For the next three years, he learned to paint and erect scenery, make props, operate a lighting board and make the best sound tapes in British theatre. As an acting assistant stage manager he was also required to 'walk on' as an actor, and gradually he got asked to play bigger parts. After working for Wolfit, he joined reps in Worthing and Leatherhead, and then in 1957 he became a member of the small guerrilla band that was Stephen Joseph's fledgeling theatre-in-the-round company, presenting summer seasons in a small room above the public library in Scarborough. Horace Ayckbourn had died earlier the same year, and Stephen Joseph became a surrogate father, giving his new disciple a lifelong enthusiasm for the 'round' and new writing as well as a maverick kind of further education in theatre and life. Joseph invited Harold Pinter, mauled by the London critics for *The Birthday Party*, to direct a production for him and Ayckbourn was deeply influenced by the older playwright's trust in what works on stage (as opposed to simply reading well, as if it were a novel) and his understanding of the way both conversation and silence can be used as weapons. He learned the power of leaving things out.

In 1959, when Ayckbourn complained that he wasn't playing interesting enough parts, Joseph told him to write a play himself; if it was any good, Joseph would put it on. The twenty-year-old Ayckbourn had just married Christine Roland when *The Square Cat*, written by the two of them under the name Roland Allen, was premièred. Joseph also encouraged Ayckbourn to direct and he made his début in 1961 with Patrick Hamilton's *Gaslight*, a play with a clever technical effect and a story involving a ruthless husband who is trying to persuade the wife he wishes to discard that she is mad. For Ayckbourn, as for his fellow actors John Osborne and Harold Pinter, the British theatre repertoire in the 1950s and 1960s was a hugely important influence, even when all three reacted angrily against it. Ayckbourn's own influences ranged in varying degree from Priestley to Pirandello, Ibsen and Chekhov, but Stephen Joseph's insistence that plays had to attract ordinary holiday-makers in from the rain and keep them engaged for a couple of hours was more influential still.

Ayckbourn gave up his job with Stephen Joseph's company after it had set up another home in Stoke-on-Trent, when the success of *Mr Whatnot* there led to its transfer to the West End in 1964. When it failed disastrously with the London critics, he took a job as a radio producer for the BBC in Leeds. Stephen Joseph died in 1967, soon after directing Ayckbourn's first major success, *Relatively Speaking*. The angry, subversive young writer gradually assumed the leadership of the Scarborough company and, apart from a two-year sabbatical at the National Theatre in the 1980s, he has been its guiding genius since 1970. In its three homes (now a splendidly converted Odeon cinema), he has directed the majority of the company's productions, set policy, raised funds, attended board meetings, negotiated with local authorities – and put aside perhaps ten per cent of his time for writing.

No theatre depends for its product and its audiences quite so heavily on its resident writer as the Stephen Joseph does on Ayckbourn. Equally, no writer relishes quite so much the challenges and opportunities which a particular theatre and a particular community offer him. He is at pains to stress that his plays are not 'tried out' in Scarborough before exploitation elsewhere; getting them right for Scarborough is the key to their universal appeal.

In 1987 Ayckbourn was appointed a Commander of the Order of the British Empire (CBE) and exactly ten years later was knighted by the Queen for services to the theatre, the first playwright to receive the honour since Terence Rattigan. His marriage to Christine Ayckbourn broke up gradually and since the early 1970s he has lived with Heather Stoney. In 1997 he and Christine divorced and he married Heather. Each, therefore, is Lady Ayckbourn: a classic piece of stagecraft.

For more details of his life, and the way it relates to his work, see my biography, *Alan Ayckbourn: Grinning at the Edge* (Methuen, 2001). Though many of his characters have been partially inspired by people in his own life, they have invariably passed through the filter of his own psyche and the creative process is generally unconscious: hence his general assertion that all his characters 'come out of me, really'. His experiments with narrative are invariably related to the content of each play rather than a conscious desire to do something different. For details of his immensely practical approach to the business of writing and directing, see his own *The Crafty Art of Playmaking* (Faber, 2002).

☞ Note

A Pocket Guide to Alan Ayckbourn's Plays includes all of his work up to the beginning of 2004. However, some of his work is not published but is still available for performance. A list of plays and publishers can be found on page 271. The early plays, which are not available for production, are discussed as a group but no details of cast lists are noted.

All the works available for performance have an easy-reference cast list denoting male and female (m and f) roles, and ages where appropriate.

The Early Plays

The Square Cat (1959), *Love After All* (1959), *Dad's Tale* (1960), *Standing Room Only* (1961), *Christmas v Mastermind* (1962), *The Sparrow* (1967)

The six plays in this section all appear in the official 'canon' of Ayckbourn's plays, but where possible all copies have been retrieved by Ayckbourn and they are not available for production. A number of other short plays were given readings or amateur productions in the period between 1959 and 1967 when these were written, a period which also included *Mr Whatnot* and *Relatively Speaking* (see below). These shorter plays have since disappeared, unmourned by the author. Those that have survived, however, are of considerable interest historically: they chart a writer's development and demonstrate the complex relationship already evident between his own life and what goes into the plays.

The collaboration between the twenty-year-old Ayckbourn, who had been working in the theatre for two years, and his slightly more experienced wife, Christine Roland, produced an unashamed vehicle for Alan as an actor. *The Square Cat*, billed as by 'Roland Allen', was largely the product of her knowledge of stagecraft and his nascent gift for plotting and dialogue. The characters lack depth but include types that would appear in full and glorious colour in more mature work. Alan played a pop star of his own age with something of his own mixed psychology: an almost embarrassing studiousness in his private persona and rampant sexuality on stage. A frustrated housewife arranges an assignation with him at an empty country house, hoping just to dance with him. Whatever he hopes for is interrupted by the arrival of her (bank manager) husband, aggressive son and attractive daughter – and the musician falls in love with the latter, who is his own age. Theatrically, the excitement for Ayckbourn was the challenge of showing both aspects of one personality, as near simultaneously as possible. Thematically, the play also deals with the disappointment of an older woman whose husband is dull and insensitive to her needs. This mirrors not only the relationship between Ayckbourn's mother and stepfather but that of Christine's parents, too.

The next two plays to be produced were also credited to 'Roland Allen'. *Love After All* featured Ayckbourn in a series of disguises as an Edwardian lover trying to make contact with the young woman whose miserly father has already allocated her to another prospective husband. *Dad's Tale* is less of a vehicle for Ayckbourn as an actor and owed its genesis to Stephen Joseph's enthusiasm for the dance company being run – in Birmingham – by Gerard Bagley. Since actors and dancers could not meet until the dress rehearsal, their work had to be entirely separate. The plot owes something to *The Borrowers* (on which a fellow Scarborough writer, David Campton, had been working and on which Ayckbourn had been intended to collaborate) and something to *A Christmas Carol*. An impoverished family has bailiffs at the door and so needs to spirit its possessions away before they can be taken; at the same time, the neighbours' Christmas dinner is delivered to them by mistake. Different versions are given of the story – another early Ayckbourn innovation – and we soon discount the idea that the family dutifully returned the turkey to the neighbours, as one of them claims. While the actors played the family and the bailiffs, the dancers were the 'tinies' who whisked things away. Dad doesn't believe in them until they turn him into a bird.

Standing Room Only is the first play to appear as 'by Alan Ayckbourn'. Stephen Joseph's strong political interests included the threats of nuclear war and of over-population. He asked Ayckbourn for something, perhaps set on Venus, about overcrowding on Earth. Ayckbourn has resisted overt political messages all his life, and came up with exactly the opposite message to the one Joseph had anticipated. He set it on Shaftesbury Avenue twenty years in the future: all traffic has long since ground to a halt and a stationary bus has become the permanent home of its driver and his family. Although there are strict regulations in force about who may or may not breed, one of the daughters defies the law by getting pregnant and the play ends up celebrating a new birth rather than restraint. Ayckbourn's instinctive resistance to the idea that governments should control lives was successful with local audiences and the producer Peter Bridge was seriously interested in transferring the play – with a star cast – to London. Somehow, a series of directors and actors failed to agree to do it, in spite of Ayckbourn rewriting it many times and reviving it successfully in Stoke.

It was in Stoke that Ayckbourn had one of his most demoralizing experiences, with the children's play *Christmas v Mastermind* (1962). Like *Dad's Tale*, it had been scheduled for Christmas in the very reasonable belief that plays should be presented for a family audience at that time. Unfortunately, elementary theatre marketing had not then been invented, and potential audiences did not know about it until after they had booked for the local pantomimes. The theatre was bitterly cold and even when audiences did come, their heavily gloved hands could not be heard clapping. Ayckbourn's tale of a dispute between Father Christmas – whose gnomes are on strike and refusing to manufacture toys – and a master criminal called The Crimson Gollywog (played by Ayckbourn himself) sank without trace and the author looked back on a career which appeared to have gone downhill since *The Square Cat*.

The Sparrow is a somewhat different case: because the two plays that preceded it (and so many that followed) were such successes, its failure to interest commercial producers is more marked. It is a somewhat downbeat play, more than usually redolent of a style abroad in the late 1960s, with echoes of Harold Pinter and many less well-remembered writers, but it still reads well and played successfully in Scarborough. It deals with two distinctly unglamorous young people, Ed and

Evie, who shelter from the rain in the flat where Ed lodges with Tony and his (temporarily absent) wife Julia. Ed is too nice or too lumpen to take advantage of Evie as she discards her wet clothes and it is the much more opportunistic Tony who captures her attention and offers her a job. But Tony is an entrepreneur who is much less than he seems, and Evie's eyes are opened to him when she sees the kind of cruel marital games he and Julia are up to, manipulating everyone else within range into complicity. Ed and Evie leave, in the rain again, turning their backs on marriage if not necessarily each other.

The Plays

Dear Reader,

Looking back over the years, I find it hard to realise that twenty-six of them have gone by since I wrote my first book—*Sister Peters in Amsterdam*. It wasn't until I started writing about her that I found that once I had started writing, nothing was going to make me stop—and at that time I had no intention of sending it to a publisher. It was my daughter who urged me to try my luck.

I shall never forget the thrill of having my first book accepted. A thrill I still get each time a new story is accepted. Writing to me is such a pleasure, and seeing a story unfolding on my old typewriter is like watching a film and wondering how it will end. Happily of course.

To have so many of my books re-published is such a delightful thing to happen and I can only hope that those who read them will share my pleasure in seeing them on the bookshelves again...and enjoy reading them.

Betty Neels

Back by Popular Demand

A collector's edition of favourite titles from one of the world's best-loved romance authors. Mills & Boon® are proud to bring back these sought after titles and present them as one cherished collection.

BETTY NEELS: COLLECTOR'S EDITION

THE FORTUNES
OF FRANCESCA

BY
BETTY NEELS

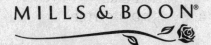
MILLS & BOON®

*MILLS & BOON and MILLS & BOON with the Rose Device
are registered trademarks of the publisher.*

*First published in Great Britain 1997 by Mills & Boon Limited,
This edition 2000
Harlequin Mills & Boon Limited,
Eton House, 18-24 Paradise Road, Richmond, Surrey TW9 1SR*

© Betty Neels 1997

ISBN 0 263 82464 0

73-0301

*Printed and bound in Spain
by Litografia Rosés S.A., Barcelona*

CHAPTER ONE

FRANNY was admitted by a butler who looked as though he hated her, shown into a small, cold room and bidden to wait there. She sat herself down on one of the stiff little chairs arranged round the table in its centre and wished that she hadn't come. The advertisement had sought a girl Friday. This term could cover anything from washing up in the kitchen to dealing with invitations on beautifully engraved cards and paying the household bills with an odd spell of babysitting when called upon. It was not what she would have chosen if given a choice, but a job and the wages which went with it had become essential.

The butler returned and frostily requested her to follow him. Crossing the hall and mounting the stairs behind him, Franny reflected that she could always refuse to take the job if she was offered it. She thrust the thought aside; common sense reminded her that she needed work.

'The young person,' said the butler, opening the double doors at the head of the stairs. Franny sailed past him. She was of medium height, rather too thin, with brown hair and ordinary features easily forgotten, but she had an air of composed dignity.

'My name is Francesca Bowen,' she said clearly, and advanced towards the occupant of the room. This was a forbidding lady if ever there was one; she was handsome, middle-aged, with rigidly controlled grey hair and a haughty nose. She looked down it now.

She gave Franny a regal nod. 'You appear very young.'

'I'm twenty-three, Lady Trumper.'

Lady Trumper hadn't expected to be answered; she looked her surprise and leafed through some letters she was holding.

'You have trained for two years as a nurse. Why did you not continue?'

'I left to look after my aunt and my brother. My aunt was ill at the time.'

'I do not require a nurse.'

'Well, I didn't suppose you did,' said Franny cheerfully, 'but you never know, it might come in useful. I can type and keep accounts, answer the phone, walk the dog, babysit...' She paused. 'I'm not a very good cook.'

'I have a cook, Miss Bowen. Nor do I require a babysitter. I am afraid that you are not suitable for the post I have in mind.'

Lady Trumper stretched out a hand and touched a bell, and the butler opened the door so quickly Franny decided that he had been standing outside listening. He preceded her down the hall with an I-told-you-so look on his face, and was on the point of ushering her out into the street when an elderly woman in a large white apron rushed into the hall.

'Mr Barker— Oh, Mr Barker, come quickly. Elsie's cut her hand that bad; she's bleeding like a pig and screaming her head off. Whatever shall I do?'

Barker said with dignity, 'I will come and see Elsie, Mrs Down, it is probably nothing more than a slight wound.'

He followed her through the baize door at the back of the hall and Franny, unnoticed for the moment, went with them.

It wasn't a slight wound; it was a nasty deep slice in poor Elsie's forearm, bleeding profusely and no one was doing anything about it.

Franny swept forward. 'Someone get a doctor or an ambulance, whichever is quickest. Clean towels and bandages, if you have them.'

Elsie's face was the colour of ashes. Franny lifted her arm above her head, found the pressure point and applied a finger, and when Mrs Down came with the towels asked, 'Can you cover the cut with several of them and press down hard? Just for a little while until help comes.' She added cheerfully to Elsie, 'It looks much worse than it is, Elsie. As soon as the doctor has seen to it, you'll feel much better. Close your eyes if you like.' She added to no one in particular, 'I hope that man hurries up…'

Mr Barker left the kitchen briskly and made for the telephone in the hall. Like so many self-important persons, he was no good at all in an emergency and, while he resented Franny's high-handedness, he felt relief at not having·to deal with the situation himself. He had his hand on the phone when the door knocker was thumped, and almost without thinking he put the phone down and opened the door.

The man who went past him into the hall was thick-set and enormously tall, with fair hair going grey at the temples and a handsome visage. He said affably, 'Anything wrong, Barker? You look a bit shaken.'

Barker took his coat. 'It's Elsie, sir. Cut herself something shocking. I am about to phone for an ambulance.'

'In the kitchen, is she?' The visitor was already at the baize door. 'I'll take a quick look, shall I?'

The kitchen was modern, all white tiles and stainless steel, and the group around the table looked all the more startling because of it: Elsie, her arm still held high, Mrs Down holding a blood-stained cloth over her arm, and a girl he didn't know applying pressure with the calm air of someone who knew what she was doing.

'Oh, sir,' cried Mrs Down as he reached the table. Franny looked up briefly.

'Are you the doctor? Good! I think perhaps it's her radial artery.'

He grunted and opened his bag, and glanced at Franny. 'Hang on until I've got the tourniquet on.'

That done, he said, 'Go on the other side of me and hold her arm steady.' He looked down at Elsie. 'I'll make you comfortable, Elsie, but I think you must go to hospital and have a stitch or two. It won't hurt, I promise you.'

'Shall I call an ambulance, sir?' asked Barker, almost his pompous self once more now that there was someone to tell him what to do.

'No. I'll take her. Someone will have to come with me.' His eyes fell on Franny. She was a nondescript girl, but she looked sensible. 'You'll come?'

Franny heard Barker's quick breath, but before he could speak she said, 'Yes, of course.' She added in her sensible way, 'Elsie will need a coat or a shawl; it's cold outside.'

An old cloak was found from behind the kitchen door and Mrs Down stood with it on her arm, looking the other way while Elsie's artery was tied off. It all took some time, what with the scrubbing of hands and the giving of a local anaesthetic into Elsie's arm. Franny, who had worked in Theatre, considered the man to be a very neat surgeon.

When the arm had been bandaged and put in a sling, and Elsie wrapped in the cloak, Franny went without fuss out of the house, walking sedately behind the doctor who was carrying Elsie.

Elsie was still feeling faint, and Franny got into the back of the car with her. She put her arm round her, reflecting that she had never expected to have the chance to travel in a Rolls-Royce. It was a pity she wasn't able to enjoy it to the full, but with Elsie shaking and sobbing it hardly seemed right to get any pleasure from it…

It was already dusk, and the chilly November day was sliding rapidly into a miserable evening. She wouldn't have to stay at the hospital, of course, but getting back home during the evening rush hour would be tedious.

They drew up outside the entrance to Casualty and the doctor got out and went inside. He returned almost immediately with a porter and a wheelchair, followed by a doctor and then a nurse. He seemed well known, thought Franny, standing quietly as Elsie was wheeled away. Everyone went with her and Franny stood undecided for a few minutes.

If the doctor had wanted her to go with him too and to stay he would have said so. Elsie was in safe hands now; Franny had no doubt that she would be kept in the hospital for the night. She turned on her heel and started for the nearest bus stop. She would have liked to have seen more of the doctor. They had hardly exchanged more than half a dozen words and she doubted very much if he would recognise her if ever they should meet again.

Franny joined the bus-stop queue and waited to begin her long journey home.

It was half an hour before Professor Marc van der Kettener came out to his car. It wasn't until he was getting into it that he remembered Franny. He went back into the hospital again to look for her, but it was quickly obvious that she hadn't waited, and he cursed himself for a thoughtless fool. She had been helpful and she hadn't fussed or asked silly questions. Why had she been at his godmother's house, anyway?

He drove himself back there, assured Barker that Elsie was quite comfortable and would be staying in hospital for a couple of days and went upstairs to see his godmother.

She offered a cheek for his kiss when he entered her quarters. 'What is all this I hear from Barker? That silly girl cutting herself...'

'I hardly think that Elsie cut herself deliberately.' The professor wandered across the room and sat down opposite Lady Trumper. 'She has quite a severe injury; she should do nothing for a week and then only light work.'

'How tiresome. I suppose Barker coped?'

'I'm sure he did his best. Fortunately, there was a young woman in the kitchen who dealt with the situation in a most sensible manner.' He glanced across at his godmother. 'A new maid?'

'Certainly not.' Lady Trumper frowned. 'Presumably Barker knew who she was?'

The professor smiled. 'Well, she was giving him orders in a brisk manner. She was brisk with me, too.'

'What was she like? Perhaps it was Mrs Down's sister...'

'Young, nice voice—educated. For the life of me I cannot remember her face. Came with me to the hospital without fuss and took herself off while I was with Elsie. Otherwise I would have brought her back here.'

Lady Trumper rang her bell, and when Barker answered bade him come in.

'Barker, do you know the young woman who helped Elsie?'

'Yes, my lady, she was the young person who came about the post you had advertised. I was on the point of seeing her out when Mrs Down came running. I had no idea that she had accompanied me to the kitchen until she took charge.' He added, 'I trust that this does not displease you, my lady? She proved herself very competent.'

'Yes, yes, Barker. She hasn't returned?'

'No, my lady. I understood that you did not engage her.'

'Very well, Barker. Thank you.'

When he had gone, she said, 'A Miss Francesca Bowen who applied for the post of girl Friday. She didn't seem quite suitable. I shall have to look for someone else.'

'No, no, Godmother. Engage the girl. She is obviously a young woman of resources and surely that is what a girl Friday should be—able to turn her hand to anything!'

'You are not serious, Marc?'

'Indeed, I am. Presumably she won't have found

another job today. Write to her and tell her that you have decided to give her a trial.'

Lady Trumper looked doubtful. 'You really think it is a good idea? But as you say, I can have her on month's trial…'

'By all means. Write her a note; I'll post it on my way to my rooms.'

'Have you patients this evening?'

'Yes, two.' He glanced at his watch. 'I had better go shortly. I'm dining out afterwards.'

Lady Trumper had gone to the writing desk under the window and picked up a pen. 'When will you be going home?'

'In several weeks. I've patients still to see and a number of theatre lists here. I have to go to Leeds and Manchester before I go back.'

'You work too hard. Isn't it time you settled down? Your dear sister mentioned someone… She hoped that you were thinking of marrying…'

'I'm afraid she must hope!' He smiled, but something in his voice stopped her from saying more. She wrote the note and handed it to him.

'Come and see me when you have time,' she begged him. 'At least let me know when you are going back to Holland.'

He bent to kiss her. 'Of course. Take care of yourself.'

Barker was waiting for him in the hall. 'Don't allow Elsie to do any work at all for several days, Barker, and see that when she does start again she keeps that arm covered. A fortunate thing that she was given such prompt first aid.' At the door he paused. 'By the way, Lady Trumper has had second thoughts and will probably engage the young woman on a trial basis.'

'We shall do our best to welcome her into the household, sir,' said Barker pompously. He added, looking almost human, 'She behaved in a most efficient manner and made no fuss.'

The professor, his mind on other matters, nodded in an absent-minded way and bade him goodnight.

Franny got off the crowded bus and turned into a side street that was badly lighted, with small terraced houses facing each other behind narrow strips of worn-out grass and battered iron railings. The houses might be small, and had seen better days, but most of them were keeping up appearances with curtained windows and cared-for front doors. Halfway down the terrace Franny opened one such door and called out as she shut it behind her. 'It's me—sorry I'm late.'

She hung her outdoor things in the narrow hall and went into the kitchen; it was a small, rather dark room, lacking the amenities often portrayed in magazines, but it was cheerful, with bright curtains and an old-fashioned red plush cloth on the table. There was a young man sitting there, books spread in front of him, writing. He said 'Hi,' as she went in but didn't look up. The elderly lady standing by the gas stove turned round to smile at her.

'What kept you, love? Would you like a cup of tea? Supper won't be for half an hour. How did you get on?'

Franny filled the kettle and put it on the gas burner.

'No good, Auntie, I wasn't suitable. It was a lovely house and there was a butler. While I was there one of the maids cut her arm quite badly so I stopped to give first aid, and when a doctor came he asked me to go to the hospital with the girl. So I did.'

'I hope that they thanked you…'

'Well, now I come to think of it, they didn't. The doctor was polite, but I think he took me for one of the servants.'

Mrs Blake looked indignant. 'Did he, indeed? What happened at the hospital?'

'Well, nothing. I mean, I didn't go in. I waited a bit but no one came out, so I caught a bus and came home.'

'Disgraceful. The ingratitude…' Mrs Blake, a small, plump lady with a mild face and grey hair, was ever more indignant.

'Well, it doesn't matter,' said Franny cheerfully. 'As we passed the supermarket in the bus I saw a notice in the window asking for check-out girls. I'll go tomorrow.'

Mrs Blake started to speak, and stopped. The gas

bill had come that morning, Finlay needed more books and the rent was due. The housekeeping money was at a very low ebb and the only solution was for Franny to get a job as soon as possible.

Mrs Blake was unhappy about that. They had just about managed while Franny had been training as a nurse; her salary and Mrs Blake's pension had kept them going. They had even been saving a tiny bit, knowing that Finn would be going to medical school when he had done so well in his A levels. He would need books and clothes and money to live on.

Then she had fallen ill. Franny had left the hospital in order to nurse her and look after the house, and their savings had gradually been eroded. Finn had now already started at medical school; there had been no question of him giving it up. He had offered to do so, and a job, any job he could get, would tide them over for a year or so, but that would have meant a year's training lost. Neither Franny nor her aunt would hear of it. They would manage, Franny had said stoutly, and, once Finn was a qualified doctor, she and auntie would become ladies of leisure. 'What is a paltry four or five years?' Franny had demanded largely.

Now they had a cheerful supper, and she took care not to mention the supermarket again. She was up early the next morning, nipping round the house, getting Finn's breakfast, taking tea up to her aunt, tidying the place, intent on getting down to the supermarket as soon as possible and getting a job.

She took her aunt's breakfast tray upstairs as usual, mindful of the doctor's advice that Mrs Blake should lead as quiet a life as possible. Having breakfast in bed was one way of doing that. Then she went to her room to get her outdoor things. She was in the hall, her hand on the door handle, when the postman pushed a letter through the letter box.

It was for her, and she opened it slowly. It didn't look like a bill—the writing was old-fashioned and spidery and the envelope was good quality...

Lady Trumper's request that she should call that morning with a view to taking up the post of girl Friday came as something of a shock. The wages she offered were even more of a shock. She would no doubt be expected to earn every penny of them, but Franny had reached the stage where she was open to any honest offer. She didn't think working for Lady Trumper would be pleasant, but the money was more important than job satisfaction. Finn could have his books and the bills could be paid.

Franny wasted a few minutes wondering why Lady Trumper had changed her mind and then went to tell her aunt.

Aunt Emma read the letter. 'Now, why would she change her mind?' she asked. 'Would it be because you gave the girl first aid?'

'That wasn't much qualification for the job, Auntie. More likely no one else has applied and she's desperate.'

'You may be right, love. You'll go?'

'Well, yes. The money is more than we hoped for, isn't it?'

'If only you could go back to hospital and finish your training…'

'I'll do that when Finn is qualified. We're managing very well, and if I went back to hospital now I'd be worrying about you all the time. The doctor said you weren't to do more than potter, and with this job I'll have plenty of time to see to the house and so on. In a month or two we'll have the bills paid and be on our feet again. What shall I wear?'

'What you wore yesterday. You looked very nice. It's raining, isn't it? A pity your mac's shabby, but you can take it off when you get there.'

'I'll do the shopping on the way home. Don't go out, Auntie, it's cold as well as wet.'

There was a faint glimmer of friendliness on the butler's face when he admitted her. 'I'm to take you straight up, miss. If you will leave your raincoat here?'

Franny followed him up the staircase. 'It's a horrid morning,' she told him chattily, 'but November nearly always is horrid, isn't it? I don't suppose you need to go out…?'

Barker turned to give her a quelling look. Familiarity was something to be nipped in the bud as soon as possible. But Franny was beaming at him and the quelling words on his lips weren't uttered.

Instead he said gravely, 'The weather is indeed in-clement.' And he proceeded on his way.

This time he announced her by name, and Lady Trumper, sitting at her desk, turned round to look at her.

'Miss Bowen, you are probably surprised to have heard from me again. I have been considering your application and have decided to offer you the post. A month's trial. I should wish you to start next Monday morning at ten o'clock. You will be ex-pected to work until five o'clock each day, but you may have Saturday and Sunday free. If I should re-quire your services at any other time I expect you to agree.'

'An annual holiday?' asked Franny.

'Oh, I suppose so. Two weeks…'

'Three,' said Franny, very politely and not waiting for a reply. 'And what exactly will my duties be?'

'Sorting my post each day and replying suitably. You said that you could type? Paying bills, checking the household accounts with Barker…'

He won't like that, reflected Franny, and gave Lady Trumper an encouraging look.

'It will be necessary from time to time to take over work from any member of my staff who is ill or on holiday. Also to arrange the flowers and see to any callers I do not wish to meet. Keep my diary cor-rectly.

'I heard from Barker that you showed a good deal of common sense when Elsie cut her hand. I shall expect you to act as nurse in the event of myself or my staff falling ill.

'You will take your meals in the small sitting room on the ground floor, but I expect you to defer to Barker, who is in charge of the household. You will be paid weekly, and if you find that you are unable to cope with the work you are at liberty to tell me and give me a week's notice.'

'Fair enough,' said Franny matter-of-factly. 'But I must point out that I have no intention of taking orders from your butler. I will respect him, and oblige him whenever possible, but I'll not take orders from him.'

She watched Lady Trumper's formidable bosom swell; she had cooked her goose, and the job so nearly hers, too. She waited quietly to be dismissed for the second time.

'I am willing to concede to your wish, Miss Bowen, as long as I have your word that you will give Barker the respect due to his position in my house. He has been with us for many years.'

'Yes, of course I'll treat him with respect,' said Franny, 'and anyone else who works here. I'll come on a month's trial, Lady Trumper.' She added cheerfully, 'I dare say we shall all get on very well together.'

Lady Trumper looked surprised. 'I trust that may be so, Miss Bowen. Good day to you; I'll expect you next Monday morning.'

She was shown out presently by Barker, who observed importantly, 'You will no doubt be joining the staff shortly, Miss Bowen?'

'Yes, on Monday morning.'

'I shall, of course, render you any assistance you may require,' said Barker at his most majestic.

'Thanks very much,' said Franny, and she skipped down the steps, turning to wave as she reached the pavement—something which took Barker aback. He wasn't a man who encouraged such behaviour. On the other hand, it was rather nice to be waved at by a young woman, even if she was without looks...

Franny squashed a desire to dance along the pavement; someone might be looking out of the window. Instead she did optimistic sums in her head and mused over ways of making the money go as far as possible. It was a good thing that Finn had his midday meal between lectures—she and Aunt Emma could eat economically and they could all eat a substantial high tea in the evening.

In the meantime, she would pop into the corner shop on her way home and get something special— bacon and half a dozen eggs, mushrooms, if there were any, and plenty of fried bread, thought Franny, her mouth watering.

Later in the evening, well-fed with these delicacies, the three of them had a light-hearted discussion about a rosy but improbable future.

At exactly ten o'clock on the Monday morning Franny presented herself to Lady Trumper. She looked neat and tidy in her navy skirt and white blouse topped by a navy cardigan. The garments did nothing to add to her looks, but Lady Trumper noticed and approved. At least the girl didn't wear a skirt up to her thighs and one of those vulgar tops printed with some stupid sentence...

'You may use the small room through that door, Miss Bowen. The post is already there; kindly open it and let me see anything of interest. And any invitations, of course.'

Hardly a task to tax her intelligence, thought Franny, dealing with the pile of envelopes with calm efficiency. She took their contents to Lady Trumper presently.

'I will read them and give you instructions as to their replies. There is a registered envelope on my writing desk. Take it to the post office. You will need money. There is a purse in the left-hand drawer—take five pounds from it and put the change into it when you return.'

So Franny got into her mac again, tied a scarf over her head, since it was drizzling with the threat of sleet, and found her way to the post office. It was quite a walk, but she needed to know a little of her surroundings. Back at the house presently, she prudently went round to the side entrance. Barker and the cook were in the kitchen. 'I came in this way because I'm wet and I might leave marks over the hall floor,' said Franny. 'May I leave my mac here to dry?'

'Certainly, and it would be convenient if you would continue to use the side door in future,' said Barker. 'Mrs Down will make coffee shortly, if you will come here when it is convenient for Lady Trumper?'

When she had gone, Mrs Down said thoughtfully, 'Not quite our sort, is she, Mr Barker? Ever so polite and nice, but I bet she's seen better days.'

'There is that possibility,' agreed Barker. 'Let us hope she remembers her position in this household.' He gave a derisive laugh. 'Girl Friday…'

If he had hoped that Franny would put a foot wrong, he was to be disappointed, for she behaved exactly as she should. The general opinion when she left the kitchen after her coffee break was that she was OK.

Queuing for her bus at the end of her first day, Franny decided that it hadn't been too bad. She had been kept busy with small jobs—none of them important, but they were time-consuming. Then the answering of letters and invitations had taken up a good deal of the afternoon, while Lady Trumper rested, but Franny had been brought up a cup of tea by Shirley, the housemaid, and had been allowed half an hour to have her dinner with the rest of the staff in the kitchen.

This had been a splendidly satisfying meal. Franny had enjoyed every mouthful, and hoped that Aunt Emma was eating the lunch she had prepared for her to heat up while giving polite replies to the questions being put to her by Mrs Down.

Mrs Down had remarked afterwards that Miss Bowen was a nice young lady, but not very forth-coming. Respectable enough, she had conceded, liv-ing with an aunt and a young brother who, Franny had told her vaguely, was studying, although she hadn't said at what.

For the rest of that week Franny found herself doing a variety of jobs. She was indeed a girl Friday: open-ing the door to callers on Barker's half-day, cooking lunch when Mrs Down was prostrated by migraine, taking charge of a toddler while his mother—a niece of Lady Trumper's—came to call. And besides all this there was the daily routine of post to be opened and answered, phone calls to take, knitting to un-ravel, bills to be paid...

At least, reflected Franny, going home tired on Friday evening, she hadn't been bored. She had a week's wages in her purse and two days to be at home. As a girl who looked on the bright side of life, Franny was happy. She hadn't been given no-tice, so presumably Lady Trumper was satisfied with her work. Franny hadn't expected to be told as much—Lady Trumper wasn't a woman to praise. After all why, that lady had often asked her nearest and dearest, should she give praise to someone who was only doing their job?

Not that Franny minded that. She didn't dislike

Lady Trumper, but neither did she like her. She was,
however, providing Franny with her bread and but-
ter…

It was during the following week that she came face
to face with the doctor who had attended to Elsie.
She had been sent to the hospital to fetch Elsie back,
for her stay there had been prolonged by an infection
which had needed treatment and antibiotics.
Although Elsie was fit to be discharged she was still
not quite herself.

Lady Trumper, wealthy though she was, was also
frugal when it came to spending money on anything
which didn't concern herself, and she bade Franny
take a bus to the hospital and procure a taxi for the
return journey, which was a brief one. And a good
thing, too, for it was another grey, damp day. Even
in this, the more elegant district of London, the
streets looked dreary. Not that Franny minded; it
meant she was out of the house for an hour.

It was a short walk from the bus stop to the hospital; she arrived at its entrance with her woolly hat
sodden on her head and the mac clinging damply to
her skirt and blouse. Her face was wet, too, as were
the odds and ends of brown hair which had escaped
from the hat. She presented not a shred of glamour,
and the professor, coming to the entrance hall as she
walked through the doors, cast an amused eye over
her person, recognising her at once.

He had told his godmother that he couldn't remember her face and realised that he had been mistaken. Though not at its best at the moment, he recalled vividly her small, unassuming nose, gently curving mouth and determined chin. It was a face redeemed from plainness by large, long-lashed eyes. Grey, he remembered.

He crossed the vast place and stopped in front of her.

'Forgive me for not knowing your name, but you were kind enough to help with Lady Trumper's maid. I had every intention of driving you back from the hospital; I should have told you so. I apologise for that.'

Franny beamed up at him. 'Oh, that didn't matter at all; there were plenty of buses. I've come to fetch Elsie back to Lady Trumper's house.'

Franny, chatty by nature, was pleased to have someone to talk to. She didn't know who he was, of course, but he had a trustworthy face. She would have embarked on an account of Elsie's accident, but was cut short when he moved a bundle of papers from one arm to the other and took a step away from her. 'Very nice meeting you, Miss—er...' he said vaguely, obviously thinking about something else.

He strode off and she wondered if he would remember that they had met again just now. She thought it unlikely. A bit vague, she reflected, but I dare say clever people often are. Being clever must make one feel lonely sometimes, living, as it were, on a higher plane than those around one. Poor man, reflected Franny, going to find out where Elsie was. It was to be hoped that he had a wife and children to keep him normal.

Professor van der Kettener, unaware of these kindly thoughts, had forgotten all about her by the time he was immersed in a bit of tricky heart surgery.

Elsie, still looking a bit washed out, was ready and waiting, eager to get back to her job. 'Not but what they weren't very kind,' she told Franny, 'but, when all's said and done, hospitals aren't like home, are they?'

When they were ready Franny hailed a taxi—much to Elsie's delight—and on their return to Lady Trumper's handed Elsie over to Mrs Down, who fussed over her in a motherly fashion, before Lady Trumper sent for her. Franny, sitting at the desk, writing invitation cards for one of Lady Trumper's bridge parties, listened to her employer laying down the law—extra care in the kitchen was required and Elsie must do her best not to be so careless.

'The kitchen is well equipped,' Lady Trumper pointed out. 'There is no excuse for carelessness. I am a most careful person myself and I expect you to be the same, Elsie. You may go.'

Franny paused in her work. She was quite sure that Lady Trumper knew nothing about knives or kitchens or being tired and sometimes overworked. She spoke her mind without stopping to think.

'I'm sure Elsie is always very careful, Lady

Trumper, but she has to handle knives and all kinds of kitchen equipment. She isn't in a position to walk away from her work if it gets too much for her. When did you last visit your kitchen, Lady Trumper?' asked Franny outrageously.

Lady Trumper had become really red in the face and needed to heave several deep breaths before she could speak. 'Miss Bowen, I can hardly believe my ears. How dare you speak to me in this fashion? The impertinence…'

'I don't intend to be impertinent, Lady Trumper, but you made Elsie feel that she had done something wrong. No one in their senses cuts themselves with a kitchen knife. But, of course, sitting here for most of the day, you would find it hard to believe that.'

'Miss Bowen, leave at once. I am very displeased with you.'

Franny gave her a thoughtful look. 'Of course you are annoyed. I expect you feel a bit guilty; one always does when one has been unfair to someone. But I'll go, although it would be sensible if I were to finish writing these cards first. Another five minutes is all I need.'

Lady Trumper took such a deep breath that her corsets creaked. 'You will go now…'

The door opened and the professor walked in.

CHAPTER TWO

THE professor looked at his godmother, whose blood pressure, he felt sure, was at a dangerous level, and then at Franny, composed and cheerful, obviously on the point of leaving.

'Am I interrupting?' he asked placidly.

'No—yes,' said Lady Trumper. 'This girl has had the impertinence to criticise my treatment of one of my maids. I have dismissed her.'

'Oh, I shouldn't do anything hastily,' said the professor. 'This is a free country in which one may express one's opinion without being flung into prison.' He turned to Franny.

'Were you deliberately rude, Miss—Miss…?'

'Bowen,' said Franny, and thought what a very large man he was—he would need a large house in which to live… 'No, I don't think so, it was just that it was something I had to say.' She added cheerfully, 'I should learn to hold my tongue, but I only pointed out that Elsie hadn't cut herself deliberately. I mean, you wouldn't, would you?' She paused. 'Well, I suppose if one were contemplating suicide… Lady Trumper was rather hard on the poor girl, although I'm sure she didn't mean to be.'

Franny gave that lady a kindly look and started to tidy the desk. 'I'll go.'

The professor crossed the room and laid a large and beautifully cared for hand over hers. 'No, no. I'm sure Lady Trumper understands now that you spoke with the best intentions.' He turned to look at his godmother. 'Is that not so, my dear?'

'Well, yes, I suppose so…'

'And Miss…' he had forgotten her name again '…is entirely satisfactory in her work?'

'Yes,' said Lady Trumper, gobbling a little.

'Then in that case is there any need to refine upon the matter? Elsie certainly had quite a severe cut, and it was unfortunate that it should have become infected. I'm sure that you will see that she does nothing to endanger her complete recovery.'

He talks like a professor, thought Franny admiringly, and with an accent, too. I wonder what it sounds like when he talks in Dutch…?

'I will overlook the matter,' said Lady Trumper grandly, 'but I must insist on no more plain speaking from Miss Bowen. My nerves are badly shaken.'

How did one shake nerves? wondered Franny. Not that Lady Trumper had any. The professor, watching her face, allowed himself a smile. He spoke quickly before she could voice her thoughts.

'I'm sure Miss Bowen will give consideration to your nerves in her future observations.' He looked at Franny. 'Is that not so, Miss—er—Bowen?'

'Oh, I'll be very careful.' Franny smiled at them

both. 'I like working for Lady Trumper and I will do my best to keep a still tongue in my head.'

This forthright speech left Lady Trumper with nothing to say and the professor said easily, 'Well, in that case, perhaps Miss Bowen might be allowed to go on with whatever she was doing while we have a little chat.'

Franny knew a hint when it was uttered. She picked up the invitation cards and went to her little cubbyhole of a room and closed the door. She had been dismissed—kindly, but dismissed, just as Elsie would have been dismissed.

And why should you mind? she asked herself. Remember that you are in a lowly position in this household. Not that it will be for always. Once Finn was a doctor with a splendid practice somewhere she would keep house for him and be respected as his sister. When he was married she would retire to a small bungalow and later live on her old-age pension.

That she had got a bit muddled in her plans for the future didn't worry her. She spent a good deal of time making plans, most of them utter rubbish and highly improbable.

She wrote another half-dozen cards and paused, struck by the thought that it would be nice to marry someone like the professor. He had everything: good looks, a successful profession—at least, she supposed that he had—and a splendid motor car. Was he married? she wondered. And what exactly did he do? Professor of what? And why was he here in England when he had a perfectly good country of his own?

Inquisitive by nature, Franny decided to find out. Franny being Franny, if she had the opportunity to ask him she would, but that wasn't likely. However a few casual questions in the kitchen over dinner tomorrow might prove fruitful...

She had finished the cards when she heard Lady Trumper's raised voice, so she opened the door and said, 'Yes, Lady Trumper?'

'You have finished the cards? Stamp the envelopes and take them to the letter box and then come back here. I want you to take some documents to my solicitor. I do not trust the post. Hand them to the senior partner, Mr Augustus Ruskin, personally, and get a receipt for them. You are to take a taxi there. You may bus back.'

'Your solicitor, Lady Trumper? Is his office close by?'

'In the City. Please don't waste any more time, Miss Bowen.'

'It will probably be after five o'clock by the time I find a bus to bring me back here. Shall I go home, Lady Trumper? Of course, if I can get back here before then I'll do so.'

Lady Trumper, who was conveyed by car whenever she wished to go out and had no idea how long a bus journey took, said severely, 'Very well. I believe that I can trust you to be honest.'

Franny said nothing. There was a great deal she would have liked to say, but she wanted to keep the job. She stamped the invitations, then wrapped in her old mac since it was raining again, posted them and went back to collect the large envelope Lady Trumper had ready for her.

'Barker tells me that taxi fares have been considerably increased. You will take ten pounds for the fare and for your bus ticket.'

Franny was soon getting into the taxi Barker had summoned and prepared to enjoy the ride. She considered that it was a lot of fuss about some papers or other; anyone else would have sent them by registered post. But since it allowed her an hour or two of freedom she wasn't going to quibble about it. The driver was a cheerful Cockney, and they enjoyed a friendly chat as he took her into London's heart. The evening rush hadn't started but the City pavements were crowded, lights shining from the vast grey buildings.

'This is where the money is,' said the cabby. 'Talking in millions behind them walls, I dare say. Pity they can't use some of it ter do a bit of work on the 'ospital. Up that lane there, St Giles'. 'Ad me appendix out there—looked after me a treat, they did.'

Franny said with real sympathy, 'Oh, poor you. Are you all right now?'

'Right as rain. 'Ere's yer office. Going back ter where I picked yer up?'

'No, I'm to go home. I work there, but I live near Waterloo Station.'

She got out and paid him and gave him a handsome tip. 'Thank you for a nice ride.'

'A pleasure—enjoyed it meself. Mind 'ow yer go. Waterloo ain't all that nice for a young lady.'

The solicitor's office was in a large grey building with an imposing entrance and a porter guarding it. 'Take the lift,' he advised her. 'Third floor—Ruskin, Ruskin and Ruskin.'

Brothers? wondered Franny, stepping gingerly into the lift and pressing a button anxiously. Or grandfather, son and grandson? Cousins…?

The lift bore her upwards smoothly and she nipped out smartly. She disliked lifts, so going back she would use the stairs.

The office was large, thickly carpeted and furnished with heavy chairs and a great many portraits—presumably of dead and gone Ruskins—on its walls. Franny made herself known to the severe lady sitting behind a desk facing the door and was asked to sit. But only for a moment, for after a word into the intercom she was bidden to go through the door behind the desk. It had MR AUGUSTUS RUSKIN in gold letters on it and when she peered round the door she saw him behind a vast desk. He must be a grandfather, even a great-grandfather, she thought. He stood up politely and she saw that he was quite shaky. But there was nothing shaky about his manner or his voice.

'Miss Bowen? You have an envelope for me? Lady Trumper informed me of it.'

He sat down again and held out a hand.

'You are Mr Augustus Ruskin?' Franny asked. 'I'm to give it only to him. Lady Trumper's orders.'

He fixed her with a sharp old eye. 'I am indeed he. You do quite right to query my identity, Miss Bowen.'

'That's all right, then,' said Franny, and handed the envelope over. 'Do I have to take any messages back?'

'Thank you. No.' He stood up again and Franny bade him a hasty goodbye, fearful that all the getting up and sitting down wouldn't do someone of his age much good. The severe lady inclined her head without looking up as Franny went past her and ran down the stairs and out into the street.

It was well past five o'clock now, and the pavements were packed with people hurrying home. She didn't know the City well and made for the nearest bus stop. There was a long queue already there and the bus timetable was miles away. If she attempted to go and look at it, the people in the queue would think that she was trying to get on first. She walked on, intent on finding someone who could tell her which bus to take, but there were no shops and no policemen. She stood on the edge of the pavement on a corner, waiting to cross the side street. She would have to take the Underground.

There was a steady stream of cars filtering from

the side street into the main street, and she waited patiently for a gap so that she could dart across, thinking longingly of her tea. Finn would be hungry, he always was, and Auntie wouldn't have bothered to eat much during the day. She would make a cheese pudding, she decided, filling, tasting and economical...

Professor van der Kettener saw her as he edged his car down the lane, away from the hospital. There she was, this very ordinary girl in her shabby mac, obviously intent on getting across the street. She looked remarkably cheerful, too. As he drew level with her, he leaned over and opened the car door.

'Jump in quickly,' he told her. 'I can't stop.'

Franny did as she was told, settled in her seat, fastened her safety belt and turned to look at him. 'How very kind. I was beginning to think that I would be there for ever. If you would put me down at the next bus stop? You don't happen to know which bus goes to Waterloo, I suppose?'

'I'm afraid not. Why do you want to go to Waterloo?'

'Well, I live fairly near the station.'

He drove smoothly past a bus stop. 'Why are you here?'

'Oh, I had to take some papers to Mr Augustus Ruskin, Lady Trumper's solicitor. Such a dear old man; he ought to have retired years ago. There's a bus stop.'

The professor said impatiently, 'I can't pull up here. I'll drive you home.'

'No, I don't think so, thank you. You sound cross. I expect you've had a busy day and you're tired. The last thing you would want to do would be to drive miles out of your way. I'm quite able to get on a bus, you know.' She sounded motherly. 'Look, there's a bus stop—if you'll stop just for a minute.'

'Certainly not. Kindly tell me where you live, Miss Bowen.'

'Twenty-nine Fish Street, just off Waterloo Road. You have to turn off into Lower Marsh. You can go over Waterloo Bridge.' She turned to smile at his severe profile. 'You can call me Franny, if you like.'

'Tell me, Miss Bowen, are you so free with your friendship with everyone you meet?'

'Goodness me, no,' said Franny chattily. 'I mean, I wouldn't dare be friendly with Barker.'

'Ah, you don't count butlers among your friends?' observed the professor nastily.

She refused to be put out. 'I don't know any, only him. At least…'

'At least what?' He was crossing Waterloo Bridge, and when she didn't answer, he asked, 'Well?'

'Nothing,' said Franny. 'It's the next turning on the right and then the third street on the right.'

Fish Street, even with the evening dark masking its shabbiness, all the same looked depressing in the light from the street lamps.

'Left or right?' asked the professor.

'The left, halfway down—here.'

He drew up smoothly, got out and opened her door. She got out too, to stand looking up into his face. 'It was very kind of you to bring me home,' said Franny. 'You need not have done it, you know, especially as you didn't want to.' She gave him a sunny smile. 'Your good deed for the day!' she told him. 'Goodnight, Professor. Go home quickly and have a good dinner; it will make you feel better.'

He towered over her. 'I have never met anyone like you before,' he said slowly. 'I trust Lady Trumper doesn't have to listen to your chatter?'

'No. No, she doesn't, I only speak when spoken to. I'm sorry if I bored you, only I thought—well, I thought you looked the kind of person one could chat with.' She crossed the narrow pavement and took out her key.

'Goodnight, Professor.' The door closed softly behind her.

The professor drove himself back over Westminster Bridge, along Whitehall, into Trafalgar Square and so into Pall Mall, going north until he reached Wimpole Street. He had a flat here, over his consulting room, for he spent a fair amount of time in London. He drove the car round to the mews behind the row of tall houses, walked back to his front door and let himself in.

The hall was narrow with the waiting room and his consulting room on one side of it. An elegant staircase led to the floor above and he took these two at a time to his own front door, just as it was opened by a rotund little man with a thatch of grey hair and a round, merry face.

He answered the professor's greeting merrily. 'A bit on the late side, aren't you, sir? But dinner's waiting for you when you want it. You're going out later—I was to remind you...'

The professor had thrown down his coat and was crossing the hall to one of the doors leading from it, his bag and a pile of letters in his hand.

'Thanks, Crisp. Dinner in ten minutes.'

His study was a comfortable room lined with bookshelves, with a fire burning in the small fireplace and a desk loaded with papers, a computer, telephone and reference books. He sat down behind it with a sigh of pleasure. This was where he would have liked to have spent his evening, writing learned articles for the medical journals, reading, going over his notes concerning his patients. If it hadn't been for that girl he would have been home an hour earlier and would have had time to finish notes for a lecture he was to give later that week. He wondered briefly why he had stopped to give her a lift. She hadn't been particularly grateful...

He dined presently, changed and went out again, this time to an evening party given by one of his colleagues. He knew many of the guests there. All of them were pleasant people, leading pleasant lives—the men in one or other of the professions, the women well-dressed, amusing, able to carry on a witty conversation. He didn't know any of them well and was unaware that he was liked. He got on well with the men and was charming to the women, but the charm hid a reserve none of them, so far, had been able to penetrate.

He left early with the plea that he needed to go back to St Giles' to check his latest patient—something which disappointed several of the women there who had made up their minds to beg him for a lift to their home.

He thought about them as he drove back towards the City. They were all delightful companions, and a delight to the eye, so why were their elegant images dimmed by the tiresome Franny with her dowdy mac and damp, untidy hair? He supposed that he must feel sorry for her. He smiled to himself; she wouldn't thank him for that. She needed no one's pity; she was one of those tiresome people who bounced back...

Auntie and Finn were in the sitting room, one with his head bowed over his books, the other silently knitting. They both looked up as she went in.

'Did I hear a car?' asked Auntie.

'Yes. A Rolls-Royce. That doctor—he's a professor—saw me as I came out of a solicitor's office in the City and gave me a lift.'

'Why were you there, dear?'

Franny explained. 'But I didn't enjoy the ride very

much. I expect he was tired after a hard day's work. He was a bit snappy. I suppose he felt that he simply had to give me a lift once he'd seen me.'

'Which Rolls was it?' asked Finn.

'Well, it was a Rolls-Royce. Aren't they all the same?'

'Not by a long chalk. What's his name, this professor?'

'Van der Kettener—he's Dutch. Perhaps that's why he's so testy...'

Finn gave her an exasperated look. 'You only had a lift with one of the best heart surgeons in Europe. He was mentioned in a lecture the other day, goes all over the place, operating and lecturing, but spends a lot of time here. He's honorary consultant in several hospitals. Lives in Holland. You lucky girl.'

Finn went back to his books and Auntie said mildly, 'Well, that's nice, isn't it, love? Such a clever man, no doubt, and yet sparing time to bring you home.'

'Pooh,' said Franny. 'With a car like that it couldn't have been a bother. I don't suppose he ever has to queue for a bus or get his own breakfast.'

'You don't like him, dear?'

She thought about that. 'I think I'm sorry for him. He was ever so—so remote. Perhaps he's quite different at home, with his wife and children. I wonder if they come over here with him, or do they live in Holland?'

She glanced at the clock. 'Heavens, is that the time? I'll get the supper. Macaroni cheese.' She paused in the doorway. 'I was going to make a cheese pudding, but the macaroni is quicker. Pay day tomorrow—I'll get fish and chips.'

Finn gave a satisfied grunt, but Auntie sighed for the days when things had been different. Not that she wasn't grateful for this poky little house in the wrong part of London, and her pension and the company of Franny and Finn. She had been a widow when they had come to live with her, and they had just lost their parents.

If only she hadn't fallen ill and Franny hadn't had to give up her nursing training to look after her and Finn. They had had plans for the future—Franny, once trained, would have found a post at some hospital in a country town, they would have lived in a small flat and managed very nicely, while Finn trained to be a doctor. With him living on his grant and any money Franny could spare, they would have made a success of things.

As it was now, they were in a cleft stick. Their combined savings were at a low ebb and there was no hope of Franny going back to the hospital; she had had to find this job where she could also cope with the house, the shopping and the cooking. Auntie had been warned that her doing anything other than the lightest of tasks might have serious consequences.

The house, which they all secretly hated, had been

offered to her at a very low rent after her husband died, by his firm, and, since there had been nothing else to do, she had accepted the offer.

Her husband, a scientist, had had a good job and they had lived pleasantly in a pretty little mews cottage in Islington. But he had been so absorbed in his work that mundane things such as life assurance or saving for a rainy day had been overlooked. Auntie had never blamed him for that—he had been a good husband—but she was thankful that they had had no children.

She put down her knitting wool and went to the kitchen to lay the table for their meal. She didn't feel very well, but there was enough for them to worry about without fussing over her. She said cheerfully, 'Tell me more about this professor—he sounds interesting.'

The next day, pay day, was the bright spot in Franny's week. One of her duties was to go to the bank each week, collect the money for the wages and hand over the little envelopes to the staff. She hadn't liked the idea of handing Barker's wages over to him; she left his envelope on the desk in her little office. It was an old-fashioned way to be paid, money in an envelope, but somehow much more satisfying than a cheque. Feeling rich, she bought the fish and chips on the way home.

They enjoyed their supper and Auntie went to bed

early. 'And don't fuss,' she begged Franny. 'I'm only a little tired.'

Franny skimmed around the kitchen, tidying it and putting everything ready for breakfast while Finn finished his studies and took himself off to his room. Once he had gone, she gave the sitting room a good clean. It was almost midnight when she went to bed and she slept at once.

She woke suddenly a couple of hours later, aware that something had disturbed her. There was a faint sound coming from her aunt's room. She got out of bed, crossed the narrow landing and opened the door.

Auntie was lying in bed, her face grey with pain and beaded with sweat. Franny lifted her very gently onto her pillows, wiped her face with a handful of sheet and said quietly, 'Lie quite still, Auntie. Finn will get the ambulance; you'll be all right—just hang on. I'll be back in a moment.'

Finn, once roused, was out of bed at once, putting on his clothes.

'Use the phone box at the end of the street,' said Franny urgently. 'Tell them it's very urgent; hurry.'

She went to her room, fetched her clothes and dressed in her aunt's room, fearful of leaving her, praying that the ambulance would be quick.

It was, and the paramedics were very competent. They wasted no time but loaded Auntie into the ambulance and Franny, leaving Finn in charge of the house, got in with them.

They worked on Auntie as the ambulance sped through the quiet streets.

'Where are we going?' asked Franny.

'No beds at St Thomas's, nor Charing Cross or the Middlesex. There's a bed at St Giles'.'

It seemed for ever before they reached the hospital but, once there, there was speed and efficiency. Surprisingly, there were no other patients in Casualty. Having given particulars in a quiet voice, Franny was told to sit and wait while Auntie was wheeled away to a cubicle at the other end of the vast place. There was a lot of coming and going then, and she longed to know what was happening behind the curtains, but she sat still, her hands folded in her lap, staring at the wall before her, not seeing it, trying not to think.

It was some time before a nurse came to tell her that her aunt was rallying under treatment. 'Sister will come and speak to you in a minute. Would you like a cup of tea?'

Franny shook her head. 'No, thank you. It doesn't matter if I stay?'

'No, of course not. Here's Sister coming now.'

Sister was young and briskly kind. 'Your aunt is improving, but until several tests have been done I can't tell you any more. She will have to be admitted, but you would have known that. It is most fortunate that the senior consultant heart surgeon is in the hospital, seeing another patient. He's on his way down now. If anyone can do anything for your aunt, it is he.'

She went away again, and presently Franny heard fresh voices and then silence, except for a murmur from time to time. Please, God, let Auntie pull through, she begged silently. And she shut her mind to a future full of problems; never mind them, just as long as Auntie got better.

Night work, thought Franny desperately. Finn would be home at least for the next few months; she could get a job, any job, which left her free during the day. She didn't need much sleep; she could shop on the way home, settle Auntie and tidy up the house and have a sleep during the afternoon...

Someone was coming towards her, disturbing her chaotic thoughts. It was Professor van der Kettener, looming large and calm and somehow reassuring. She sat up straight and said, 'Hello, Professor,' in a tired voice.

He stood looking down at her. How this girl dogged his footsteps, he thought. As usual she was looking rather the worse for wear. It was understandable, of course, in the circumstances, and her hair, hanging down her back in a pale brown tangle, bore witness to the fact that she had dressed in a tearing hurry. But she was looking up at him with a brave, hopeful face.

He sat down beside her. 'Your aunt is gravely ill. She has an atrial septal defect—I'll explain that presently. It can be put right with open heart surgery.

Before that is done there are a number of tests to be carried out to confirm those which have been done now. She will be admitted into one of my beds and in due course I will operate. It is a serious operation, but she is a resolute lady, isn't she? If all goes well I can see no reason why she shouldn't return to a normal life.'

He looked at her. 'You do understand what I am saying?'

'Yes, thank you. Is she to be warded now? May I see her first, before I go home?'

'Certainly you may. Come with me.'

She went with him and he held the curtains back for her as she went into the cubicle. Auntie was conscious. She looked small and very frail, but she smiled at Franny.

'What a fuss and bother,' she whispered. 'So sorry, love.'

'You'll be comfy in bed very soon, Auntie, and you're going to be well again. Professor van der Kettener says so. I'm going home now but I'll be here tomorrow—in the afternoon, I expect. I'll bring the things you'll need with me.'

She bent and kissed her aunt and went back through the curtains to where the professor was waiting, talking to the sister. There were porters already there, with a stretcher and trolley, and a nurse and a young doctor.

Sister turned to look at her and said kindly, 'Would you like a cup of tea now? Do you have far to go?' She glanced at the clock. 'It's almost four o'clock. I dare say there'll be a night bus... Or have you someone you can phone to come for you?'

'I'm fine, thank you, Sister. May I come tomorrow afternoon?'

'Of course. Go to Reception, and they'll tell you where your aunt is. Have we got your phone number?'

'We haven't a phone. I'll ring about eight o'clock.'

Franny smiled vaguely at them both and turned away, but was brought to a halt by the professor's firm hand.

'I'm going your way; I'll drop you off.'

He kept his hand there while he exchanged goodbyes with Sister and had a word with the young doctor who had come across to speak to him, and only then took it away.

Going out of the casualty entrance, Franny said uncertainly, 'But I'm not on your way. Besides, you have been up almost all night, haven't you? You must be tired. I can get a taxi...'

He took her arm and trotted her across the forecourt to his parked car.

'Don't talk rubbish. Have you any money with you?'

'No.'

'So stop making difficulties where there are none. Get in, do!'

She got in and he closed the door on her, got in

himself and drove off through the quiet streets. It was very dark and, save for the milk floats and an occasional car, the streets were empty. In another few hours they would be teeming with traffic.

The professor drove without speaking, but his silence didn't bother Franny—indeed, she was glad of it. She was tired but there would be a good deal of arranging to see to. She tried her best to think sensibly about that, but she wasn't very successful.

Her muddled thoughts were disturbed finally by the professor.

'When you get home, have a warm drink and go to bed even if it is only for an hour or so. Later on you'll find you can think clearly again. And don't worry too much about the future. One thing at a time. Is there anyone at home now?'

'My brother.' She needed to add to that, 'He's a medical student, just started.'

'Good.' They were crossing Waterloo Bridge, and in a few minutes she would be home. 'I'll come in with you, if I may?'

She couldn't think why he wanted to do that, but she was too weary and worried to think about it. She said politely, 'I dare say you would like a cup of tea.'

He stopped outside her home, got out and came to open her door. Finn was waiting for them on the doorstep.

The professor nodded at him. 'You don't mind if I come in for a few minutes?'

'No, no, of course not, sir. Franny, is Auntie OK?'

Franny looked at the professor. 'You tell him. I'll put the kettle on.'

A little later they sat, the three of them, round the kitchen table with mugs of strong tea and a packet of Rich Tea biscuits, and the professor won a life-long devoted friend in Finn because he treated him as an equal while he explained exactly what needed to be done for Auntie. He spoke with self-assurance and cheer, promising nothing but offering hope, and Franny, listening to his quiet voice with its almost imperceptible accent, took heart. Then he paused to say, 'Would you not like to go to your bed? I'll be off in a few minutes.'

He stood up and she got to her feet, wished her goodnight and thanked her for his tea.

'It was very kind of you to bring me home,' said Franny, her eyes huge in her tired face. 'I hope you will go home to bed, too. And do drive carefully.'

He told her gravely that he would.

Franny tumbled into bed after setting the alarm for eight o'clock. Though it was Saturday, she'd been summoned to be at Lady Trumper's by ten o'clock. At all costs she must carry on with her job there. They were going to need every penny she could earn...

Before she dropped off to sleep she remembered what the professor had said about one thing at a time. She would do that.

At eight she got up and found Finn already in the

kitchen, making toast. He looked up as she went in
and gave her a cheerful grin. 'Auntie's OK. Resting,
they said.'

'You went to the phone box?'

'No. Professor van der Kettener is quite a man,
isn't he? Left me his mobile phone. Told me to keep
it until we got sorted out.'

He took it from his pocket. 'See? We can phone
the hospital whenever we want to.'

Franny was overcome with gratitude and a warm,
comfortable feeling that someone was helping them,
but, she added to that, only until they could help
themselves.

She looked much as usual when she presented herself in Lady Trumper's sitting room. Opening Lady
Trumper's post, Franny was thankful that it was
Saturday. She would go to the hospital in the afternoon, and later she and Finn would sit down together
and decide what was best to be done.

Lady Trumper, voice raised impatiently, wanted
to know why she was so slow. 'And you look as
though you haven't slept. I hope you're not one of
those girls who burns the candle at both ends?'

Franny held her tongue. Her head ached and she
was deeply worried about Auntie. A good cry would
have helped, preferably on an understanding and reassuring chest. The professor would have done very
nicely, only he didn't like her.

CHAPTER THREE

AUNTIE was holding her own. Franny sat beside her bed in the intensive care unit, holding a limp hand and making cheerful remarks from time to time so that Auntie could see that she wasn't worried about anything at all. And Auntie dozed, waking every now and then to ask anxious questions in a small, breathy voice.

Professor van der Kettener had been to see her that morning, Sister told Franny, and had been pleased with her condition. There were to be more tests but, if they were satisfactory, he would operate as soon as possible.

'And afterwards?' Franny asked. 'I mean, will my aunt be in need of constant nursing? Could she be left at all?'

'There should be very little nursing needed, and I would suppose that she could be left safely for quite long periods.' Sister looked at Franny. 'What kind of work do you do, Miss Bowen?'

'Well, at present I work for someone during the day, but I wondered if I should get a night job. I've got a brother who is still living at home, so he could be there at night and I'd be home during the day. I

52

know I'd have to sleep for part of the time, but Auntie would know that she wasn't alone.'

'That seems quite a good idea. Are you trained for anything?'

'I've had two years' training as a nurse, but I gave it up to look after my aunt and run the house. I had to be home, you see…' Franny added cheerfully, 'I manage quite well and I've no doubt we can arrange something later on.'

'There is no possibility of going back to hospital?'

'Not for the moment.'

Sister said thoughtfully, 'Perhaps we might be able to get your aunt a bed in a long-stay hospital.'

'She would die,' said Franny simply. 'Besides, she has given my brother and me a home, and now it's my turn to look after her.' She added firmly, 'Everything will be all right, Sister, and I'm so happy to see her looking better. May I come again tomorrow? I'll bring my brother with me.'

That evening, sitting over their supper, she and Finn laid their plans. It would be three weeks before Auntie could return home.

'So I'll stay with Lady Trumper for as long as possible,' said Franny, 'but in the meantime I'll look for a night job—perhaps a nursing home not too far away. The pay won't be too bad; we can manage.'

Finn began, 'I could get a job—'

'No, dear, that's the last resort, and things aren't all that desperate.'

Which wasn't quite true, she reflected uneasily,

what with the gas bill due to be paid and the rent, modest though it was, to be paid, too. And food. Franny thought that she could save quite a bit on that. Finn needed a good cooked breakfast, but she could tell him that she was slimming. Just for a while, she told herself, until she could get some money saved.

'We could write to Uncle William,' suggested Finn.

'Him? I'd rather die, and you know you would, too.'   'But he was our mother's brother—he can't still be angry because she married Father. It's years ago…'

'Yes, but he swore that he never wanted to see her again and he would have nothing to do with us when they were killed in that accident. He always thought that Mother had married beneath her, although of course that wasn't true. And remember how badly he has treated Auntie, just because she went to their wedding and kept in such close touch?'

'But now Auntie is so ill surely he would help her?'

'Finn, until we are absolutely desperate, I want nothing to do with Uncle William. He's mean and disagreeable. When Mother and Father died and Auntie wrote and told him, he sent her letter back torn into little pieces. It's a pity that Father hasn't any family still living.'

She began to collect up the supper dishes. 'You

are not to worry, Finn, everything's going to be all right.'

She didn't tell him that she had called in at the supermarket on the way home and got herself a job stacking shelves from eight o'clock until ten each evening.

Christmas was near enough for a demand for casual labour. They'd been only too glad to take her on and, when she explained that she might have to give up the job quickly, they had agreed to that too. The money wasn't much, but if Auntie was going to be in hospital for at least three weeks she could save every penny of it.

It was several days before Sister told her that her aunt was considered fit enough for an operation.

'Professor van der Kettener will be doing it, so your aunt has every chance of a complete recovery. He is a quite famous surgeon, you know. He is going back to Holland for Christmas, but by then your aunt should be well on the way to recovery. Since she is elderly she may have to stay in hospital for a few days longer than usual, but of course we shall let you know her progress.' Sister smiled at her. 'It's a worrying time for you, isn't it? You look tired; are you sleeping well?'

'Yes, thank you, Sister. I am worried, of course, but I'm sure everything is going to be all right. It would be nice to have Auntie home for Christmas; do you think that will be possible?'

'Perhaps—but that is more than three weeks away. That's something for the professor to decide before he goes. He will operate in two days' time and I'm sure he will leave instructions to his registrar to tell you exactly how things are. He might even have time to see you himself.'

On the day of the operation Franny went straight to the hospital from Lady Trumper's house. Auntie was conscious, looking very small, in a bed in Intensive Care hung around with tubes and apparatus vital to her recovery. She smiled at Franny, and said in a whisper, 'I'm back, dear,' then dozed off again.

Franny sat beside her for a long time, holding her hand, her head empty of thought. She was tired, and she hadn't slept well for the last two nights, but she intended to stay for as long as she would be allowed. From time to time a nurse came to check everything, smiling kindly at her, offering whispered suggestions that she might like to go and get a cup of tea or coffee, but Franny shook her head. A young doctor came, too, telling her that she need not leave while he was there.

'Just keeping an eye on your aunt,' he told her cheerfully, but presently the door at the far end of the ward opened and Sister came in with the same young doctor, an older man and Professor van der Kettener. Franny did get up then, and went and stood at one of the windows, looking out at the street below without seeing it.

It was ten minutes or more before the group around her aunt's bed dispersed and the professor came over to her.

'I am very satisfied with your aunt's condition,' he told her without preamble. 'She will sleep throughout the night and will be well cared for. You must be tired; I suggest that you go home and have a good night's sleep and telephone in the morning.'

Franny looked up into his face, trying to read the thoughts behind its calm expression. 'You say that you are satisfied with Auntie's condition. I want to know if the operation was a success, and will she be quite well again? And how long will she be here? And, when she comes home, will she need nursing?'

He frowned down at her. 'It is early days to expect answers to those questions, Miss Bowen. I can assure you that the operation was entirely successful. I have closed the opening—it was a large one—between the atria. There is a certain amount of hypertension which will improve. Your aunt will come off the ventilator within the next twenty-four hours. As you are no doubt aware, all necessary recordings will be taken half-hourly and, of course, the ECG monitor will be continuously watched. I assure you that every care will be taken.'

'Yes, I'm sure of that. I didn't mean to be nosy…'

'I understand your anxiety. Your aunt will probably be here for three weeks—rather longer than a younger patient—but by the time she returns home she will be able to lead a quiet, normal life. No need for nursing. In any case, visits from the practice nurse in your area will be arranged.'

'Thank you for sparing the time to tell me,' said Franny. 'I'm sure you're very busy.'

He smiled a little, gave her a little nod and went away. He was preoccupied, but he spared the time to think about Franny's pale, tired face. Too pale and too tired, he reflected, but not in the least defeated. Perhaps some kind of help could be arranged when her aunt returned home. It was obvious to him that there wasn't much money. It would be better if Franny were to stay home when her aunt returned, which would mean giving up her job...

He went out to his car and drove himself home, and forgot about her.

Franny, making her way back to Fish Street some time later, hadn't exactly forgotten him, for he had this tiresome way of popping into her thoughts at the most unexpected moments, but she had a great deal else to think about. Later that evening as she stacked shelves with washing powder, tinned fruit and endless cans of soup, she was still making plans and rejecting them.

If Auntie was to stay in hospital for three weeks Franny would be able to work at the supermarket until then, but after that things might be a bit difficult. Lady Trumper wasn't likely to let her stay away from her work. She would have to leave, but not before finding other work. Her nursing training would stand her in good stead; nursing homes often employed women with nursing experience even if they weren't qualified. And night work was never popular.

True, the area around Fish Street wasn't likely to yield much in the way of nursing homes—the people who lived in that area went to hospital or died in their beds—but if she could find something not too far away from home... Surely there were dozens of homes catering for the elderly and infirm.

Franny, released from her shelves, went home and outlined her plans to Finn.

Auntie began to recover slowly. There was nothing to worry about, Sister told Franny, the professor was pleased with her progress. 'And he did say that he thought she might be well enough to go home for Christmas.'

Franny, loading her shelves with Christmas puddings, crackers and iced cakes, had time to plan for the festive season. She and Finn had already turned the sitting room into a bedroom for Auntie, only to be told by Sister that Auntie would need to take exercise and going up and down to bed would be good for her. So they rearranged everything once more and Franny set about getting in a stock of food; from time to time the supermarket staff were allowed to buy things at a reduced price.

'A great help,' she told Finn over supper. 'We can get biscuits and things in packets,' she explained.

She worked out a routine for herself and, although she had no leisure and not enough sleep, she managed very well. Lady Trumper eyed her once or twice and remarked that she would do well to lead a more sensible life.

'What you young women get up to in your leisure is no concern of mine as long as it does not affect your efficiency,' she'd said. She went on, 'And don't expect more than two days off at Christmas. It is an especially busy time for me—extra entertaining and countless letters to write. Which reminds me, you will have to go to my dressmaker and fetch a dress she has ready. You had better take a bus, and kindly do not waste time on the way.'

As Christmas approached, Franny's days got busier. Lady Trumper might complain about the buying of presents, entertaining of guests and the invitations which she accepted, but she saw to it that the fatigue was taken out of these exertions by enlisting the help of those around her. She might spend a morning buying presents, but it was Franny who wrapped them up, labelled them and wrote the recipient's name. And it was Franny who trotted to and fro the post office, wrote invitation cards and answered the door when Barker or the maids were busy or off duty.

Looking at her reflection in the mirror in her bedroom one evening, she could see that she had never looked so plain.

Professor van der Kettener, coming to the hospital to take a look at Auntie before he left for Holland, would undoubtedly have agreed with her. He came quietly onto the ward, walking its length to where Auntie sat in a chair by her bed. She was fairly active now, up and about for most of the day, but now, in the quiet hour after supper, she was enjoying a visit from Franny. She looked up with a delighted smile as he reached her.

'Professor, how nice to see you. I thought you would be back in Holland…'

'I'm going tomorrow morning. I wanted to pay you a last visit, which I can do while you are here in hospital, Mrs Blake. You will be going home in a few days now, but I shall want to see you when I come back. I'll ask Sister to arrange for the hospital car service to bring you to my clinic.' He looked at Franny then. 'You will be glad to have Mrs Blake home again. Don't let her do too much over Christmas.' He added casually, 'I shall be leaving in half an hour or so; I'll give you a lift home.'

Franny said, 'How kind, but there's really no need; there are plenty of buses. I'm sure you have a great deal to do, especially as you're going away tomorrow.'

'I will be outside the main entrance in half an hour, Franny.' He nodded briefly, shook hands with his patient and went away.

'Now that is kind of him,' observed Auntie. 'A very thoughtful man. He's very well liked here, you know. Never throws his weight about but nonetheless everyone does what he asks them to do without a murmur. A nice man,' concluded Auntie. 'I hope he has a very happy Christmas.'

Listening to this, Franny thought that she had better do as the professor asked too; he would be quite capable of sending someone to fetch her if she didn't present herself at the entrance at the right time. Besides, it would be delightful to be driven back sitting in the comfort of the Rolls-Royce. The buses would be crowded and would take a long time. With any luck, she would have time to sit down and have a cup of tea before going to the supermarket.

The Rolls was parked just outside the entrance, with the professor in it. He got out as Franny went through the doors and went round the car to open its door for her.

'This is very kind of you,' observed Franny chattily. 'The buses do take a long time.' When he didn't reply she added, 'I expect you're excited at the idea of going home...?'

The professor, who hadn't been excited about anything for quite a few years, grunted.

'Christmas is such a nice time,' went on Franny, refusing to give up. 'I expect you have your family waiting for you?'

'Myself and my family can be of little interest to you, Miss Bowen.' His voice was cold.

'Well, I like to know about people,' she told him. 'Don't you?'

'Only in so far as it concerns their health.'

Franny sniffed the nice leathery smell of the car.

'How dull,' she said cheerfully. 'I dare say you'll feel better when you get home; you must get tired with so many patients.'

'Not only the patients tire me, Miss Bowen.'

He sounded sarcastic and she said at once, 'Oh, you mean me? I'm talking too much, I'm sorry.'

So for the rest of the journey she didn't utter a word. Only when he drew up in Fish Street did she thank him politely, and wish him a happy Christmas.

'Are you not going to ask me in for a cup of coffee?' he asked, to surprise her.

'Well, of course. Only I didn't ask you because you seemed a bit—cross—no—tired. But, please, do come in. Finn will be home; he's one of your fans.'

The professor got out of the car and stood beside her on the pavement.

'I thought only pop groups had fans.'

He followed her into the narrow hall, talking, and taking up almost all the space. Franny edged round him.

'Come into the sitting room,' she said, and raising her voice she called, 'Finn, Professor van der Kettener has come for a cup of coffee.'

She ushered him in and left him with Finn while she went to the kitchen and put the kettle on, laid the tray and found the biscuits. There was almost an hour before she had to go to the supermarket, which would be time enough; the professor wouldn't stay long.

In this she was mistaken. The hour was almost up

and he was still sitting there, discussing the functions of the heart with an enraptured Finn. What was more, he showed no signs of going, so that in desperation Franny was forced to get to her feet. When he started to do the same, she said, 'No, don't get up, there's no need. But I—I have to go out, so I'll say goodnight.'

The professor raised an enquiring eyebrow and looked—most unfairly, she considered—at Finn.

'Franny stacks the shelves at the supermarket for a couple of hours each evening.' He added uncomfortably, 'I wanted to do it, but she insists that I must study.'

The professor nodded and smiled, and Finn gave him a relieved grin.

'You are still working for Lady Trumper?' he asked Franny.

He asked so nicely that she said readily, 'Oh, yes, it's not hard work at all—and—and I like to keep busy.' She gave him a cheerful smile. 'Finn will make some more coffee, so don't hurry away unless you want to.'

'When do you come back?'

'About ten o'clock.' She whisked herself through the door and out of the house.

Stacking shelves didn't need a great mental effort but it was tiring. When her shift was finished Franny walked the short distance home in the company of two other girls living in the same street, and felt quite unreasonable disappointment when she saw the Rolls had gone.

She let herself in and at once took a great sniffing breath, for the delightful smell of fish and chips filled the house. She bounced into the sitting room and found Finn still at his books. He looked up as she went in and grinned.

'I say, the professor's a splendid chap—he went and fetched fish and chips because he said he'd missed lunch and couldn't wait to go home for his supper. He brought enough for you; it's in the oven, keeping hot.'

'Fish and chips,' echoed Franny. 'Not in a paper bag from the place at the end of the street? I mean, he didn't actually go himself?'

'Yes, he did. He may be getting on a bit, but he's not in the least stuffy.'

'He's not old,' said Franny, and went to get her supper. It was delicious, the chips crisp and very hot and the fish—plaice in a thin batter crust—mouthwatering. Much tastier than the hake she had always bought because it was the cheapest...

She went back into the sitting room. 'Where did you eat?' she asked.

'Oh, here. I fetched a couple of plates and knives and forks. You see, he was explaining the technique of bypassing.'

'Well, I expect it was an experience for him,' said Franny, gobbling chips.

* * *

The professor, eating his dinner with rather less than his usual appetite, met Crisp's reproachful gaze. 'Circumstances forced me to have a meal of fish and chips not an hour ago, Crisp. They have taken the edge off my appetite.'

'Fish and chips? Not, I trust, from one of those shops where they are wrapped in paper?'

'Well, yes, although they were put into bags first.'

'I trust you will take no harm from the food, sir.' Crisp sounded disapproving. 'I take it that it was necessary for you to actually eat it?'

'Oh, yes. I really had no option and I enjoyed it— although, of course, there was no comparison with the delicious meals you cook, Crisp.'

Crisp allowed himself a wintry smile and went away to fetch the coffee. 'Most peculiar,' he told his cat, Trimble. He was a large tabby cat who had moved in with him, a lean and hungry stray, although anyone looking at him now would never have believed that. 'Acting so strange,' went on Crisp, picking up the coffee tray. 'He must have had a reason. Fish and chips, indeed!'

Trimble, a cat who knew on which side his bread was buttered, looked intelligent, and Crisp nodded at him. 'See what I mean?'

It was a pity the professor was going to Holland for Christmas, for there would be little chance of Crisp discovering the reason behind his actions. By the time he got back he would have forgotten all about it.

But for the moment the memory of his evening spent at Fish Street was very clear in the professor's mind. The shabbiness of the little house was etched clearly in his head—and not only the shabbiness, but the neatness and spotlessness of its furnishings, and Franny's matter-of-fact cheerfulness. Christmas would be a sober occasion for them, and he could see no way of making it more festive.

It would be simple enough to send a Christmas hamper anonymously, but Franny would very likely suspect him of sending it, for as far as he knew there was no one else likely to do so.

He went to his study and began to clear his desk, preparatory to leaving in the morning, but Franny's unremarkable face kept getting between him and the papers there. There must be some way in which he could make sure that some Christmas fare got into Fish Street. A way which would make it impossible for Franny to refuse it. He had no doubt that if she knew that he had sent it she would more than likely send the box of goodies back, however tempting they were. She wasn't a girl to accept charity meekly.

The solution came to him so suddenly he was surprised he hadn't thought of it before. He glanced at his watch and saw that there was still time to make a phone call...

Two days before Christmas Eve, Auntie was discharged from hospital. She sat, her goodbyes said, by her bed, waiting for the hospital car service to come and collect her. She had listened carefully to the advice the nice young doctor who had been looking after her had given her, thanked Sister and the nurses and handed over the box of chocolates Franny had wrapped in festive paper. The unexpected appearance of Sister surprised her.

'Mrs Blake, I've a surprise for you. While you were ill we had a lottery in the hospital and we took a ticket for you.' She smiled widely at Auntie. 'And guess what? You have won the first prize.'

And she handed Auntie a large shopping basket wrapped in Cellophane, filled to overflowing with packets and jars and tins.

'I'm sure your niece will have arranged a marvellous Christmas for you, but I dare say you can use some of these things.'

'I won this?' Auntie was almost tearful. 'Sister, how lovely! How very lucky I am; we shall enjoy all of it. But I must owe you for the lottery ticket...'

'No, no.' Sister improvised quickly. 'We get tickets for all the patients who aren't able to do so for themselves.' Hopefully, she reflected, Mrs Blake wouldn't give the matter too much thought. And Auntie didn't; being guileless herself, she never suspected guile in others.

She was driven back to Fish Street presently, to be welcomed by Franny and Finn. The driver of the car said that he couldn't spare the time for a cup of tea, so Auntie was borne indoors, sat down by the fire and given tea and crumpets while they all talked at once.

It was mid-afternoon; Lady Trumper had grudgingly conceded her a half-day, and Franny didn't need to go to the supermarket for some hours, and Finn had put away his books for a while. Tea finished, Franny drew a small table to Auntie's chair, put the prize basket on it and handed her the scissors to cut the Cellophane.

The contents were a magnificent collection of extravagances: tea—not tea bags but elegant little tins of Earl Grey, finest Assam, Orange Pekoe—little sachets of cappuccino coffee, glass jars of pâté, smoked salmon, Parma ham, chicken in aspic, a box of crackers, a small Christmas pudding, a fruit cake, crystallised fruits, a box of chocolates, a trifle, Stilton cheese, biscuits—plain and sweet—and half a bottle of champagne.

Franny arranged everything on the table and sat back to look at them.

'It's like a dream,' she said happily. 'We're going to have a splendid Christmas. I've ordered a chicken and I'll get some salad. What a wonderful prize. Did any of the other patients win anything?'

'I don't know, dear. I was so taken by surprise. It was almost worth going to hospital...' Auntie laughed at her little joke.

On Christmas Eve Franny went to Lady Trumper's as usual, and despite the dark, miserable morning and the ill-tempered people on the bus she was happy. Auntie was home and well again, Finn had done well at medical school and they had the where-withal to enjoy a happy Christmas. Barker's grumpy face did nothing to dampen her good spirits, and even the half-hearted thanks she received from him and the rest of the staff when she gave them the small gifts she had got for them was no more than a momentary disappointment.

A little seasonal good feeling would have been nice, but, although the house was decorated lavishly with holly and tinsel and a big tree in the hall, Lady Trumper evidently didn't allow the Christmas spirit to go further than the outward show. She found fault all day with Franny, bemoaned the fact that she was forced to have friends in for drinks that evening and professed angry astonishment at the size of the bills which had come by the morning's post.

'The amount of money I am forced to spend,' she told Franny. 'The bills can be paid after Christmas; let them wait for their money.' She saw Franny's look of disgust. 'I suppose you think that I should pay promptly? Those kind of people spend their money on rubbish and drink, anyway.'

Franny couldn't let that pass. 'Yes, I do think that you should pay your debts to people who have earned the money and need it to live on. People have children and old people to look after, schools to pay for. And I dare say they spend a great deal less on drink than you and your friends, Lady Trumper.

There's a bill for champagne—a dozen bottles at more than twenty pounds a bottle—that would keep a large family in food and drink for two weeks at least.' She added for good measure, 'And by drink I mean tea and coffee and the occasional beer.'

Lady Trumper was having difficulty with her breathing. 'You insolent girl,' she managed finally. 'You can clear your things and go now. I am only sorry that I ever listened to Professor van der Kettener.'

'Well, I thought that would be what you would say,' said Franny. She had lost her job but for the moment she couldn't care less; she had only spoken her mind. Everyone in a free world was entitled to have their own opinion. She began to tidy the desk where she was writing place cards for the Christmas dinner party. 'I've worked for two and a half days...' She did some sums on the back of an envelope. 'That works out at...'

Lady Trumper snapped, 'I shan't pay you a penny.'

'Then I shall have to take you to court,' said Franny in a reasonable way.

Lady Trumper stared at her. She said, 'Take what is owing you from the desk.'

Franny thanked her, counted out the notes and showed them to Lady Trumper. 'I hope you'll find someone you'll like,' she said. 'And I hope you have a very happy Christmas, Lady Trumper.'

She left the room quietly, went down to the

kitchen to wish everyone there goodbye, and, while they were still exclaiming their surprise, she left the house.

There was no need to tell Auntie and Finn that she had lost her job—she would have been free for a few days, anyway, over Christmas and once it was over she could break the news and find something else. Night duty, she mused as she was squashed between two men reading newspapers on the bus. It shouldn't be too difficult to get work—indeed, she had been thinking about it ever since she had known that Auntie would be coming home and would need an eye kept on her.

'One door shuts and another one opens,' said Franny, speaking her thought out loud so that the two men lowered their newspapers and glared at her.

She wished the bus conductor a merry Christmas as she got off the bus and made for Fish Street. She would have to go to the supermarket later on, but first they would have tea and hot buttered toast round the fire and then she would make a steak and kidney pudding, warming and filling.

She went past the fish and chip shop, closed now until six o'clock, and the sight of it reminded her of the professor. He'll be surrounded by family by now, reflected Franny. There will be a tree, and the women will be dressed up and there will be children—well, if he's married there will—or perhaps a fiancée—and later they'll sit down to a magnificent feast...

*   *   *

Which was exactly what the professor was doing. He had gathered his family around him as he did each year, and now he was sitting at the head of the vast mahogany table, a host to his three sisters and brother, their husbands and wife, and a clutch of children. He sat, listening to the babble of cheerful voices around him, joining in the talk from time to time while he thought about Franny.

It was, he admitted to himself, neither the time nor the place to think of her, but she had become firmly rooted in his head. He supposed it was because he felt sorry for her; certainly he admired her cheerful outlook on life even though she hadn't much to be cheerful about. Despite his Christmas hamper, he didn't suppose that Christmas would be all it should be for her.

He glanced round the room and wondered what she would think of it. It was a vast apartment, with panelled walls and a high ceiling. There was a fireplace at one end of it and three tall windows hung with dark red velvet curtains along one wall, facing a vast serving table laden with silver. The floor was highly polished wood partly covered by an Aubusson carpet, echoing the red of the curtains.

The table gleamed with silver and crystal and delft blue china, with a central floral arrangement of holly and Christmas roses, hyacinths, lilac and narcissi. The chandelier above it blazed down on the seventeen people sitting there—the smaller children perched on cushions, the youngest of all in a highchair. This was a traditional meal which the family observed each year.

Tomorrow, Christmas Day, there would be a family lunch, of course, after church, but the rest of the day would be given over to the children, with presents from the tree and games and later, when the children were in bed, a buffet supper for the grown-ups.

The youngest of his sisters, Sutske, broke into his thoughts.

'Marc, do you suppose that next Christmas you will have a wife to sit at the foot of the table?' She spoke half-jokingly. She was his favourite sister and made no bones about poking her nose into his life.

He said lightly, 'I have no plans to marry, my dear, but I am told by my registrar at St Giles' that love comes unasked. And he should know; he has just become engaged and is determined that everyone around him should be in the same state of bliss!' He laughed then. 'So probably I shall take you all by surprise.'

There was a lot of light-hearted banter after that, but presently the talk turned to family affairs, and later, when the children had been put to bed, there were friends who had been invited for the evening.

The professor, wandering among his guests, didn't think about Franny at all. Only much later, when everyone else had gone to bed, he sat in his study with Biddy, his golden Labrador, sprawled over his feet, and found himself wondering what Franny was doing.

CHAPTER FOUR

FRANNY was lying in her bed, plotting ways and means. She was by no means downcast—supper, augmented with a few extras from Auntie's prize, had been a satisfying meal. The supermarket manager had added a box of biscuits to her pay packet that evening and she was free for two days. She was concocting answers to the offer of work she felt sure she would get, and on this hopeful note she went to sleep.

If she thought of the professor at all during the next two days she didn't allow her thoughts to linger on him. She listened to Auntie's warm praise of him because she had no choice in the matter, but she made a point of thinking of him as he was in the hospital—kind and impersonal, a man who probably was just as kind and impersonal to hundreds of other anxious relatives. That there was another side to him, the side which allowed him to buy fish and chips in paper, one which she would like to know more of, was best ignored.

So Christmas was happy, after all. Going to bed on Boxing night, Franny allowed herself a few minutes in which to think about him. She thought it was unlikely that she would see him again, and if she did it would be at his clinic when she took Auntie for her check-up. There would be no chance to talk to him, and anyway, she reminded herself, there had been various occasions when he had expressed irritation with her chatter. Better if she never saw him again. Perhaps Finn could get time off to take his aunt…

Christmas over, she set about the urgent task of finding work. A study of the situations vacant columns in the various newspapers at the local library was encouraging. Any number of residential homes, rest homes and nursing homes were seeking helpers. But most of them were too far from Fish Street to make it possible to reach them within the hour. Besides, there would be the bus fares… She picked out several possible vacancies just across the river and went home and wrote letters applying for each of them. Only when she had done that did she tell Auntie.

'I've been wanting to change jobs,' she told her airily, 'and I like night duty. And when Lady Trumper gave me the sack I was delighted, for it saved me having to give her notice…'

Auntie looked doubtfully at her. 'Really, love? You aren't doing this because I've come home?'

'Good heavens, no!' said Franny, and sounded so convincing that she quite believed it herself.

She had answers from three of the advertisements. They were all from nursing homes for the elderly and the nearest one was in Pimlico, a fairly short and simple bus ride over Lambeth Bridge. The letter was vague as to duties, and didn't mention a salary, but it said that she would work for five nights each week, eight o'clock in the evening until eight o'clock in the morning. An interview was suggested, if she would telephone and make an appointment.

At least I can go and see what it's like, reflected Franny, and went out to the phone box at the end of the street.

She went to the home the next morning, carefully timing the bus ride and the walk of several minutes to the nursing home, which was quite large. At one time it must have been a handsome town house, but now it looked a little bleak, with heavy curtains at the windows and a notice by the door bidding callers to ring twice, and tradesmen to go the side door.

Franny rang twice and was admitted by a young maid in a brown overall suffering from a heavy cold, then ushered into an austere room leading from the hall, and asked to wait. The room was chilly and felt damp. Franny supposed that it was seldom used—certainly there was nothing in it to tempt its occupiers to stay longer than necessary.

The maid came back in a few minutes and led her across the hall into a room overlooking the street. It was well furnished as an office, cosily warm, with a couple of comfortable chairs, a TV in one corner and a tray of coffee set out invitingly on a side table.

The woman behind the desk wasn't what Franny

had been expecting; she was young—in her early thirties—smartly dressed and skilfully made-up. Her hair, worn in a fashionable straight cut with a fringe, made Franny, with her wealth of hair in a chignon, feel old-fashioned.

'Miss Bowen?' A well-kept hand was held out. 'I am Mrs Kemp; please sit down.' She turned over several papers before her. 'You have references?' When Franny handed them over she quickly read them and said, 'They seem satisfactory. Are you free to join my staff immediately? As I wrote in my letter, you will work for five nights of the week. There are eighteen patients here and at night there is a registered nurse in charge, with yourself as her aide. I see that you are not qualified, so your wages will be those of an untrained worker.'

She mentioned a sum which Franny knew was less than it should have been, but even so it was sufficient to keep them provided they were careful—and the job did have the advantage of not being far from home. She said nothing and Mrs Kemp went on, 'You will have an hour off during the night—three quarters of it for your meal and a quarter of an hour for your tea break. You won't need uniform; I provide overalls for the staff. If you would like to work here I will ask someone to show you round. You do realise that our patients are elderly and for the most part infirm?'

She touched the bell on her desk and Franny was led away by a middle-aged woman whose replies to

Franny's cheerful queries and remarks were so taciturn that Franny gave up presently and contented herself with having a good look round, aware that her companion didn't like her lingering too long in any of the rooms.

Most of them held four beds, all neatly made. A few rooms were single or with two beds, and there was a day room with easy chairs, all occupied by ladies in various stages of old age. None of them were doing anything, although the television was on and there was a table with books and magazines on it.

'You'd better come and see the kitchen,' said her companion finally. 'You'll be making hot drinks and getting breakfasts there.'

It was a depressing place, thought Franny—eighteen old ladies sitting silently doing nothing. She hoped that their families came to see them often and that there was a good doctor.

She went back to Mrs Kemp presently and told her that she would take the job.

'Very well, Miss Bowen. A week's notice on either side. You pay for breakages, of course, and I expect that you will be punctual.'

'Your patients…' said Franny. 'Do they just sit all day? I mean, are none of them able to go out or walk about a bit? And does the doctor visit regularly?'

Mrs Kemp smiled brilliantly. She hoped this girl wasn't going to be too good at her job. The nursing home was doing very nicely, and with the minimum of staff she employed there was little chance of doing more for the patients than keeping them clean and fed and getting them in and out of their beds.

She said now, 'Indeed, they are free to go wherever they wish. And, of course, their families take them out, and we have a splendid doctor. Of course, you aren't likely to see the patients other than in bed.'

She took up some papers from her desk. 'I shall expect you tomorrow evening, Miss Bowen.'

The woman who had shown Franny round came then, and went with her to the door. She wished her a rather surly goodbye and closed the door before she could reply.

Not ideal, thought Franny, waiting for her bus, but there were advantages—regular pay and an easy journey to and from work. She didn't look further than that; it would be too depressing.

She enlarged upon the advantages of the job that evening, so that Auntie and Finn felt quite satisfied about it, and the following evening she went off to work.

She was admitted by the same dour woman, led to a small cloakroom and given her overall. She was given a nurse's cap too. 'The patients like to think you're a proper nurse,' said the woman seriously. 'That'll make you look professional.'

There was no sign of Mrs Kemp, and when Franny asked if she was to see her before she started work she was told she wasn't there. 'Gone to the theatre—she and Mr Kemp enjoy a good play.'

'So who's in charge?' asked Franny.

'Sister Payne, she'll be upstairs.'

On the first floor there was a small room, presumably for the use of the staff. A middle-aged, rather stout woman was sitting there, drinking a cup of coffee. She looked up as Franny went in and smiled.

'You're the new nurse? Nice to meet you.' She held out a hand. 'I'm Becky Payne. Have a cup of coffee and we'll have a chat.'

Franny sat. Mrs Payne looked friendly and she had a pleasant face. The other woman went away without speaking and Mrs Payne said, 'You don't need to bother about her. She's the housekeeper—does the cooking and runs the place. There are two women who come to clean each day...'

'And the nursing staff?' asked Franny.

'Well, now, they come and go. This isn't a place to attract young nurses. Mrs Wright—the day sister—she runs the place during the day, and there's two aides full-time and a part-timer, and then there's us.'

'But who takes over when we have our two nights off?'

Mrs Payne looked surprised. 'Didn't Mrs Kemp tell you? We relieve each other. It's a bit of a scramble on your own, but we've always managed. It means starting the day early in the morning, but no one's ill; it's just a question of keeping them clean and comfy.'

Franny asked, 'Supposing someone is taken ill, who must I tell?'

'Dr Trevor. Don't disturb the Kemps. They've got the flat at the top of the house.' Mrs Payne said comfortably, 'Don't worry, love. It's an easy job as jobs go. Wouldn't suit everyone, but I dare say it's what you were looking for.'

'Yes,' said Franny. 'I have to do night duty so that I can be home during the day.'

Mrs Payne didn't ask questions. 'Now, we'll go over the list of patients and then we'll go round together and make sure that everyone is comfortable. Mrs Wright has given them their sleeping pills. She's a registered nurse…'

'We don't need to give them medicine, then?'

'No. Nothing prescribed, just cough medicine and inhalations and suchlike.'

They stood up and Franny tugged her overall into a more comfortable fit. It was over-large and bunchy round the waist. 'Is Mrs Kemp a registered nurse?'

'Yes. Has to be, doesn't she? But she never sets foot outside her office.' Mrs Payne smiled and winked. 'This place is a gold mine; she's in it for the money. You'd be surprised at the number of people prepared to pay high fees to have Granny or Mother stashed away.'

She led the way into the first room and the night's work began.

They took it in turns to have their meal during the night, which had been left to keep warm, presumably by the housekeeper, and was eaten in the kitchen. They made their own tea in the early hours, drinking it together in the duty room. Franny was surprised at the lack of care needed for the patients. They slept soundly until she went round rousing them at seven o'clock with early-morning tea. It was when she was reading the charts she found in the duty room that she discovered that they were all on sleeping pills.

'Do they need them?' she asked Mrs Payne as they went to and fro with the patients' breakfast trays.

Mrs Payne laughed. 'I doubt it, but who am I to worry about that? If they all sleep all night, you see, there's no need for a lot of nurses, is there?'

'What do they do during the day? Several of the ladies seem quite active.'

'Well, there's the telly, isn't there? And some of them have a newspaper. They're well fed and kept clean. Look, ducks, they're old. I've been nursing geriatrics for years. Hospitals don't have the staff or the money to do more for them. I've worked in homes like this one for a long time now, and this one is not bad compared with some I've worked at. Don't you worry your head about it. No one's unkind to the patients here, I can promise you that. Now here's Mrs Wright; we can be off in ten minutes…'

Mrs Wright was middle-aged, too, and she looked nice. Franny was careful to address her as 'Sister' and felt better about the patients; she looked kind and efficient and it was obvious that the two young assistants stood in some awe of her. Franny took herself off home, reflecting that so far the job was at least what she had hoped it would be. She wasn't very happy about the patients, but they seemed content... Early days, she reminded herself.

She settled down quickly and, although the work wasn't hard, it was necessary to keep awake and alert throughout the night—and two of those nights she was alone. Washing and feeding eighteen old ladies took time, and she wasn't a girl to cut corners. She went back to Fish Street each morning, tired to the bone, to take Auntie her breakfast in bed and get herself a meal.

To cook was too much of an effort, so she made tea and ate a slice of toast, tidied the house and prepared lunch, before having a shower. In her dressing gown, she saw Auntie safely into the sitting room, had coffee with her and then got her a light meal.

'You must eat something,' Auntie always said worriedly, but Franny always declared that she had had a huge meal at the nursing home.

'I'll cook something when I get up,' she'd assure her. 'I'm going to bed now, but you're to wake me if you don't feel well or you need me. I'll leave the door open. The tea tray is ready if you fancy a cup before I get down.'

She would leave Auntie sitting by the gas fire with her knitting and her books and take herself off to bed. It seemed to her that she had no sooner put her head on the pillow than the alarm went off and she had to get up again. A cup of tea and then a meal shared with Auntie and Finn revived her; she told herself that life wasn't bad at all, and she had two days off to look forward to.

By the end of the second week she had got into a routine which she told herself was admirable. The two days off were a godsend; she was able to shop, clean the house, have two nights' sleep in her bed, sit by the fire and listen to Auntie reminiscing about her youth and hear Finn's sparse accounts of his days. She was content, she told herself, but she didn't dare to look too far ahead.

It was during the third week of her work at the nursing home that Auntie had an appointment to go to St Giles' for a check-up. There was no indication as to who would see her, but all the same, just in case it would be the professor, Franny persuaded Finn to take an afternoon off and accompany his aunt. She tried not to think too much about the professor, aware that she was finding it difficult to forget him. To see him again would be pointless and foolish, would reawaken her wish to get to know him. She saw Auntie and Finn off and after an early lunch took herself off to bed.

The professor's clinic was busier than ever, so Auntie waited patiently for her turn, aware that Finn wanted to get back to his books. She suggested that he might see the professor, but Finn shook his head. 'No way—he's here to see his patients. He wouldn't have time for me.'

But the professor did have time. While he examined Auntie he asked a few questions—was she quite happy to be back home? Was she doing as he had told her, leading a very gentle way of life? Was Franny with her?

Auntie said yes, and then added, 'Franny isn't with me. Finn brought me; Franny's in bed.'

'Ill?' The professor's voice was sharp.

'No, no. She's doing night duty.' Auntie waxed garrulous. 'The dear child works at night so that she can be in the house with me during the day. Finn's at home at night, of course.'

The professor looked up from the notes he was writing. 'I thought Franny was at Lady Trumper's.'

'She left. I believe she annoyed Lady Trumper in some way.'

The professor reflected that that was very likely. 'She is quite happy with her present job?'

Auntie was cautious. 'Well, she doesn't say much about it. It seems rather a sad sort of place and she seems to be on her own a great deal.'

'I dare say it's close by Fish Street?' asked the professor casually.

'A short bus ride.' Auntie was sitting back, enjoying the pleasant gossip. She didn't see Sister's impatient look and the professor ignored it. 'Eighteen patients—not your kind of patient, though. Old ladies—not ill, exactly, but there because it's convenient for their families.'

'I occasionally get called out to a nursing home, but I don't recall visiting this one...'

'Pimlico,' said Auntie. 'It's called The Haven.'

'Most appropriate,' observed the professor as he smiled at Auntie very kindly. 'But home is best, is it not?'

'Indeed, it is. May I know if I'm quite well again? Shall I be able to do a little more? It would be such a help if I could just do the shopping and some of the housework.'

'It is still early days, Mrs Blake, but by all means start doing light jobs around the house. But only for short periods—and you must rest as much as possible. Do you sleep well?'

'Like a top,' said Auntie.

He got up and shook hands. 'I'd like to see you again, of course. Will you go to Reception? They will give you a date. Is Finn in the waiting room?'

When Auntie said that he was there, the professor walked with her. To Sister's indignation, the other patients' interest and to Finn's huge and inarticulate delight, he spent a few minutes with him asking him about his studies.

It was late afternoon by the time they got home, and Franny was up, still in her dressing gown, getting tea. She listened to all that they had to tell her, careful not to ask any questions about the professor, and Auntie quite forgot to tell her that she had told him where Franny was working. She thought about that later and decided that perhaps she shouldn't have done so. It would be better to say nothing…

The professor never overlooked even the smallest detail. He had asked Auntie how many nights in the week Franny worked and she had told him, adding for good measure on which nights she was free. He would go and see her, he reflected, merely to satisfy himself that she had a good job and was able to give Auntie the care she still needed—Auntie was his patient and he was responsible for her welfare.

It was some days before the opportunity occurred for him to go and see her. Given an early breakfast by Crisp, who contained his curiosity with difficulty, he drove himself to The Haven and parked a few yards from it. He watched three women—the day staff, he presumed—go in, and then an older woman leave, and, a moment later, Franny.

She was not looking her best, he perceived at once. Indeed, studying her as he eased the car forward, he saw that her face wasn't only plain, it was without color, and thin. When he was alongside her he opened the door.

'Get in,' he told her, and because she was surprised she did.

Only, once sitting beside him, she said sharply, 'No, I don't want to. I'm going home.'

He leaned over and fastened her seat belt. 'Good morning, Franny, I'll drive you home.'

'Why are you here?'

'I wanted to talk to you.'

'Auntie? Is there something wrong? What's happened?'

'Nothing. Your aunt is doing very nicely—making splendid progress. I wished to see for myself that you were able to cope.'

'Well, that's different. Everything's fine. This is a nice job and I get plenty of time off to see to the house and Auntie. I'm sorry I upset Lady Trumper— I didn't mean to—but it was a good thing, really, because I had to find another job.' She turned a tired face with an over-cheerful smile to him. 'I get two free days a week and the pay's quite good.'

'Good. How many patients are there at this place?'

'Eighteen. They're not ill, only old and shaky and needing care.'

'How many nurses do you have at night?'

'Well, there's me and then there's Mrs Payne...'

'And who else? Who relieves for nights off?'

'Oh, well—we relieve each other.'

'And then you are alone? All night?' They had crossed the bridge and were almost at Fish Street. 'You wash and feed all the patients before you hand over in the morning?'

'Yes. Professor, why are you so interested? Anyway, now you know, don't you?'

He drew up soundlessly before her door. 'Now I know that you are overworked, Franny, not getting enough help or sleep or exercise, and you are beginning to look like a small scarecrow.'

She had been glad to see him, though too tired to respond to him, but now she sat up straight and turned an indignant face to his.

'Whatever next? Scarecrow, indeed! I was beginning to think you were rather nice, but you're not.' She made to get out of the car but his hand over hers prevented that. 'I'm very grateful for all you've done for Auntie,' she added rather stiffly. 'But I assure you that I'm quite capable of looking after her and running my own life. Thank you for the lift.'

He got out of the car and opened her door. 'I've made you angry. I'm sorry. Forget about not liking me and listen to me as you would listen to your doctor. Think about finding work away from London if you can. Somewhere where Auntie can potter gently in the garden and you can work where you have a chance to meet people and enjoy your life. The life you lead now is nothing but genteel slavery. Goodbye, Franny.'

She didn't reply. Suddenly she wanted to tell him just how awful the job was, how tired she was, how life seemed an endless round of work, shopping, and seeing to Auntie and the house. Even with Finn, who did his best.

She mumbled something, still not looking at him, opened the door and went inside, closing it quietly behind her. It had taken an effort to do that; what she had really wanted to do was throw herself onto his massive chest and bawl her eyes out in comfort.

Finn wasn't home and Auntie was in bed. She sniffed away her tears and began the morning chores—tea for Auntie and a cup for herself, breakfast, the sitting room to tidy and dust, the kitchen to clear, lunch to think about, shopping… Another day in a succession of days which stretched into the future.

She stopped laying Auntie's tray. The professor had said that Auntie would be better out of London—well, there were jobs all over the country and it was worth thinking about it.

During the next few days she thought a very great deal about the future. To move right away from London would be a tremendous upheaval. Finn would have to get digs—though she didn't think he would mind that. He would see more of his friends and feel free to spend his leisure as he wanted and not feel that he must stay at home at night and help with the chores. As for Auntie, Franny thought that once she got used to the idea she would like it. This house was rented, and probably they could find something as cheap or cheaper out of London. Besides, she herself might find work which was better paid…

She searched the columns of *The Lady* magazine, for people wanting help in the house, help with children, carers for elderly members of the family. I won't hurry, Franny told herself, I'll wait until just the right kind of job turns up—not too far away from London and Finn, somewhere where I can get to work easily, where a house or a flat goes with the job, and where there is a mild social life for Auntie such as the Women's Institute or a special club.

Full of optimism, she didn't allow herself to think of her own future. During the scant moments of peace and quiet at the nursing home she thought about the professor. He had washed his hands of her and she deserved it. She had been ungrateful and rude and she would forget him just as he surely must have forgotten her.

A week or two went by, and now that she had made up her mind Franny set about looking for a job in real earnest, though she still said nothing to Finn or Auntie. Time enough for that when she had found what she wanted. There had been three likely jobs in Kent, Sussex and Surrey, and she had written to all three; it seemed there was nothing to stop her careful planning.

However, there was. Auntie caught a cold which became a chill—nothing to worry about, her doctor assured her, but she was to stay in bed until she had taken the antibiotics he had prescribed and not go out of doors until the weather improved.

Franny managed somehow to go to work, do the shopping and keep the house tidy, but she had to cut her sleep to a few hours during the day. She was anxious about Auntie, and anxious, too, that nothing should interrupt Finn's studies.

It was becoming evident to her that Auntie needed more care than she was getting. However caring Franny was, she needed someone there all the time. Franny wished there was someone in whom she could confide. The professor would have done nicely, she thought ruefully, but dismissed him impatiently from her mind. 'Stand on your own two feet, my girl, and don't moan,' she told herself.

Auntie made slow progress, but after a few days she came downstairs, looking pale and frail and a bit peevish. She made no bones about broaching a subject Franny had avoided. 'This can't go on, Franny,' said Auntie weakly. 'You're doing too much and we have to put a stop to it. I've been thinking that I might go into a home...'

'Don't you even dare think about it. This is your home, Auntie, and you made it home for Finn and me. I'm perfectly all right and you're getting better each day.'

'Well, something must be done,' said Auntie obstinately. 'I don't intend—' She was interrupted by a knock at the door, and Franny, glad to put an end to the conversation, went to open it.

Uncle William stood there, supported by gutter crutches, and his wife, Aunt Editha. He was a short, stout man with a red face made fierce by bushy eyebrows and a perpetual frown, and, when he spoke, he had a harsh voice.

'Well, girl, don't just stand there, let me in.'

Uncle William was a man whom no one liked, with the possible exception of his wife. He was considerably older than Auntie and Franny's mother and had already been a spoilt and bad-tempered boy when they were born. Since his doting parents had turned a blind eye on his bullying ways and arrogance they had fallen victim to his domineering ways. Not that the two girls had been meek about that—they had stood up to him valiantly and on one occasion had belaboured him so furiously that he had tripped and fallen. The consequence had been a black eye, a broken nose and several front teeth knocked out.

The two girls had been severely punished but he had been the laughing stock of the other young men of his acquaintance. He had vowed then that he would never forgive them and that somehow, some day, however long it took, he would get even with them.

The opportunity had come sooner than expected; their parents had died within weeks of each other and he had become the family's guardian.

Auntie had escaped first, marrying a man against her brother's wishes, but since she had been twenty-one he had been able to do nothing about it. And then Franny's mother had been fortunate enough to meet a man when she was nineteen who had married her out of hand, despite William's efforts to prevent him.

Franny, aware from childhood of Uncle William's nasty nature, and regarding him as a kind of family ogre, now stifled a nasty feeling of foreboding and held the door wide.

'You're a surprise, Uncle William.' She nodded at her aunt, who was a thin, middle-aged lady elegantly dressed in a beautiful winter coat which Franny instantly coveted. 'And you, too, Aunt.'

She led them into the sitting room where Auntie, wrapped in a rather tatty shawl, sat by the fire. She had started to doze, and now when she opened her eyes she stared and closed them again. Franny, aware that she was shutting out the unwelcome sight of her brother, touched her gently on the arm.

'Auntie, here are Uncle William and Aunt Editha. I don't know why they have come, but I dare say we shall be told.'

She offered chairs, ignoring Aunt Editha's shuddering looks at the room. 'Finn is in medical school; he'll be home later.'

Her uncle spoke. 'Don't take after your mother, do you? She was pretty... What do you do with yourself? Don't look too healthy to me.'

'I am very well. If you are at all interested in the matter, Auntie has had a recent heart operation and is recovering nicely.' Franny eyed him with dislike. 'Why are you here, Uncle, after all these years of ignoring us? For all you might have known, we could have been dead or emigrated.'

Auntie was wide awake now. She said, still feeling

peevish, 'Indeed, yes. A fine brother you've been to me, and uncaring of your nephew and niece—your own flesh and blood, too.' She turned an indignant eye on her sister-in-law. 'And you're no better.'

Aunt Editha looked astonished, as well she might. Auntie had never spoken to her like that before—of course, she was getting on; old people tended to forget themselves. She opened her mouth to reply but Uncle William forestalled her. 'That is why we are here.' He attempted to soften his voice. 'To make amends.'

He paused, but if he expected looks of gratitude he didn't get them. He waited for a moment and then went on. 'Editha and I have decided that we should give you a home. I can see that you, Emma, are greatly in need of one. Is this house yours?'

'No, William. My husband's firm allows me to rent it. I have a home, thank you, and I have no wish to live with you and Editha.'

'I've taken you by surprise. You must have time to think things over. There is a home for Francesca, too, and, of course, Finlay when he is free from his studies.'

'Where would we live?' asked Franny.

'With us in Dorset, of course. I may say it's a delightful house, may I not, Editha, without boasting? A pleasant social life, fresh country air, good food.' Uncle William, carried away by his own words, added, 'You would have every care and attention, Emma, and I'm sure that Francesca would find plenty to occupy her and an opportunity to meet people of her own kind.'

Franny said, 'I'm sure you mean it kindly, Uncle, but it's rather late in the day. We have made a happy life for ourselves here. Finn is doing well, Auntie is making a splendid recovery and I have a good job.'

She glanced at Auntie, who nodded agreement. 'I'll get tea. I'm sure you'd like a cup before you go.'

It wasn't very polite, but Uncle William had never bothered to be polite when they had needed help and been ignored.

Presently Uncle William drank his tea, shaking his head sorrowfully from time to time, while Aunt Editha asked searching questions which Franny answered with a regrettable lack of truth. When they got up to go at last, she expected that Uncle William would renew his offer, but all he said was, 'You mark my words, you will be glad of my generosity. I have not taken umbrage; I shall offer you a home again if and when it is necessary.'

With which pompous speech he took himself off with Aunt Editha in tow, out of the house to the waiting car—an old-fashioned Daimler with a chauffeur. Franny watched them drive away and went back to Auntie.

'Whatever has come over your uncle?' Auntie wanted to know. 'After all these years, too. You don't suppose that we should do as he asks, Franny?

You wouldn't need to work, and you'd have young friends and some decent clothes...'

Franny collected up the tea things. 'I'm very happy as I am, Auntie. You don't want to go, do you?'

'No, love. It would have to be something beyond our powers to make us go.'

Four days later, plodding down Fish Street after a long and busy night, Franny slipped on an icy patch and sprained her ankle. The milkman, trundling past on his float, stopped, scooped her up and took her home. He phoned the doctor, too, who came some time later and examined her poor swollen ankle. He strapped it, told her not to walk on it, wrote an X-ray form for her and arranged for her to be taken to hospital. She had to wait there for some time and later, reassured that it was just a sprain which would heal itself with rest, she was sent back home again. She must see her doctor in a few days time, the casualty officer had said kindly, and take care not to put any weight on the foot.

It was the kind of nightmare Franny had always steadfastly refused to encourage. Even with painkillers the pain was severe, but, despite the doctor's instructions, there were times when she had to disobey him. Finn was a tower of strength when he was home, but, despite Franny's efforts, Auntie insisted on doing a lot of things she had no business to do. It was a relief when Franny, conveyed to the doctor's surgery on the back of Finn's old bike, was given permission to be prudently active. She hobbled into the house, feeling that the worst was over.

Only it wasn't. There was a letter from Mrs Kemp in answer to the one Franny had sent to her. She regretted Franny's accident but was sure that Franny would agree with her that she would be unable to keep her job open any longer—the temporary nurse who had taken over was quite willing to remain. A week's wages were enclosed.

'Well,' said Franny, rather too loudly and cheerfully, 'things couldn't be any worse; they can only get better.'

It seemed that she was wrong. She had just put the letter down on the kitchen table when someone thumped the door knocker and she hobbled to open it. It was Uncle William.

CHAPTER FIVE

THE professor, immersed in his work, found to his annoyance that Franny's face, so lacking in looks and now so hard to forget, had imposed itself upon his mind. He must, he decided, go and see her again so that he might reassure himself that she was of no importance to him whatever. His temper, quite a nasty one, which he had learned to keep under control, was increasingly tetchy so that even the faithful Crisp asked him anxiously if he was working too hard. 'Perhaps a few days off, sir?' suggested Crisp.

The look of affront which he cast at the professor's terse reply caused the professor to say quickly, 'Sorry, Crisp. I've something on my mind—it makes me irritable.'

Crisp accepted the apology with dignity and told Trimble later that doubtless the professor was planning one of those tricky operations of his. The professor was actually planning his next few days' workload—and not only work; he had numerous friends and a number of evening engagements. In a couple of days' time, he reflected, he could give himself a free afternoon…

A plan he was forced to discard. He received an urgent summons to Brussels where a VIP had had a heart attack and the professor's advice and probable surgery were top priority. He was there for three days, decided to operate in a week's time, and flew back to London where a backlog of work awaited him. To visit Franny was out of the question, although his personal inclination was to go and see her. He could, of course, phone her at the nursing home, but he guessed that her nights were busy enough without added interruptions. He thought of writing, but he had no idea what he wanted to say.

At the end of the week he went back to Brussels and, since the VIP was an ill man and the operation a serious one, he stayed there until his patient was on the road to recovery. And, once more back at St Giles', he worked his way through theatre lists, ward rounds and clinics. Only when he had cleared his desk of most of his work did he turn his thoughts to Franny once more.

A great deal was happening at Fish Street. Uncle William had taken matters into his own hands while Franny, feeling too ill to stop him, nonetheless had done her best to reject his plans.

She had very little help from Auntie, who could only express relief that her brother had offered them a home again and that their troubles were over. Nothing Franny could say would persuade her that everything would be all right in a few weeks. For once Auntie was firm.

'You're talking nonsense, love. I'm useless, and

don't you pretend otherwise. You're unable to work, let alone look after me and shop and cook and see to the house. You know better than I that while you have to hobble around like that your ankle won't mend completely, and until it does you can't get a job. I know you don't like your uncle. Nor do I. But he is family and he has offered us a home. And it need not be for always.'

'Finn...I can't leave him. Where will he go if you give up this house?'

Finn, to her surprise, sided with Auntie. 'I know we all dislike Uncle William, but we can't go on like this, Franny. Even if I gave up and got a job it wouldn't be enough to keep us, and you can't work and look after the house and Auntie.' He gave her a brotherly look. 'You do look a bit of a wreck, you know, and that ankle isn't getting a fair chance...'

'But what about you?'

He grinned. 'A bit of luck. Josh—remember I told you about him?—he and two other men have found a flat and they're looking for a fourth to share. It won't cost much—I'll get a job washing up at one of the hotels...'

'Indeed, you will not,' said Auntie. 'I shall sell this furniture and one or two things I don't need and you will take the money...' She saw Finn's mouth open to protest. 'As a loan. It should be sufficient to keep you going for a few months while you see if you can get a bigger grant...'

So very much against her will Franny gave in.

Despite Auntie's belief that Uncle William had turned over a new leaf and was prepared to make amends, Franny didn't believe that; she neither liked nor trusted her uncle. He had turned his back on them when her parents had died, declaring he wanted nothing to do with them, and now suddenly out of the blue here he was, taking over their lives. Why?

And he wasn't wasting time. Having wrung their agreement to his plans, he was arranging everything with ruthless efficiency. Auntie had given up the house, a firm had sent a man to look over the furniture, they were to be driven down to Dorset in a week's time. Their small household bills were paid, Finn moved in with his friends... At least he was all right, thought Franny. Auntie had given him enough money to see him over the next few months.

'For we shan't need much money,' she had declared cheerfully, 'and I have my pension. I dare say William will give you an allowance.'

Franny didn't say anything. If Uncle William gave her money she would throw it back at him. It was bad enough having to live on his charity, for that was what it was—he wasn't doing it from love. So why was he doing it?

She pointed out to him that Auntie was still an out-patient at St Giles' and needed to have regular check-ups. 'I'll write and explain,' she told her uncle. 'But you do understand that she will need to go up to the hospital at regular intervals? I'll write to her doctor, too...'

Uncle William, paying one of his brief visits to make sure that they were doing everything he had laid down, took out his notebook. 'Give me the names of these doctors and the hospital departments and I will see that they are informed. I will give them my home address so that they can contact your aunt. I will also explain matters to our own doctor, a very good man, who can get in touch with these hospital people so that your aunt has the best possible treatment.'

Franny, surprised at his concern, agreed, stifling a feeling that Uncle William was turning out to be too good to be true. She wished now, as she had wished every night in her bed, that she could have seen the professor. The wish became so strong that she actually went down the street to the phone box and rang the hospital and asked to speak to him, only to be told that he was in Belgium. When she enquired as to when he would return she was told that that wasn't known. 'Is it urgent? Concerning a patient of his?' she was asked.

'Yes, but it's not urgent.' She hung up and went back home. Perhaps it was as well that he hadn't been there, for what would she have said? It was of no interest to him where she and Auntie lived. Auntie had been his patient. He knew that she had a home and someone to look after her and would have dismissed her from his mind until he might at some future date see her at one of his clinics. Perhaps, she thought wistfully, he would be told of

Auntie's new address... And then what? Franny asked herself. Did she really think that he would do anything about it? Of course not.

Uncle William lived in a small Dorset village some miles north of Wimborne, and although Franny had never been there she knew quite a bit about it, for her mother had described it to her many times and Auntie liked to recall her childhood there.

After Franny's mother and father had married, they had never gone back. Uncle William, having recently taken over the house from his dead father, had made it plain that his young sister—since she had chosen to marry a mere schoolmaster—would no longer be welcome there. When Franny had written to tell him of her parents' death, he had sent the letter back, torn up, washing his hands of both her and Finn. It had been Auntie, recently widowed, and equally ostracised by her brother, who had given them a home.

Packing the last of their clothes, Franny wondered again why Uncle William had had a change of heart.

It was hard to say goodbye to Finn but, as they reminded each other, she would be coming up to London from time to time when Auntie was due for a check-up, and Uncle William might invite him down to Dorset. She would miss Finn but she had the good sense to see that he would enjoy being independent. Perhaps once Auntie was settled in and happy and being well looked after she could find another job, but that was something she must keep for the future…

Uncle William sent a car for them, driven by a morose man who had little to say for himself, merely volunteering his name—Hancock, Uncle William's chauffeur—settling them in the back and driving away without loss of time.

Auntie was excited, and Franny persuaded her to sit back and close her eyes. She still looked very fragile and Franny worried about her, but now perhaps she would get back to her former reasonable health—obviously life at Uncle William's was going to be very different from Fish Street. Franny, easing her still aching ankle from its shoe, felt hopeful.

Brinsleigh Court, a pleasant Georgian house, stood on the edge of Brinsleigh village. As the car turned into its gateway, Auntie said, 'I never expected to see my home again. I'm so happy that you are coming here to live, Franny.' She sighed. 'I have so many happy memories.'

And some unhappy ones, too, reflected Franny, although she didn't say so.

They got out of the car and Hancock took their luggage from the boot. The big door under the porch had been shut, but now it was opened and a tall, stout woman ushered them inside.

She greeted them politely in a cold voice. 'I'm Mrs Beck, the housekeeper. You will want to go to your rooms. Lunch has been delayed and will be served in half an hour in the dining room.'

If Auntie had expected a warm welcome, then she was disappointed. She acknowledged the house-keeper's words with a dignified nod and asked, 'Is Lady Meredith not at home?'

'She will join you at lunch.'

Franny, going slowly up the stairs, her arm around her aunt, didn't look at Mrs Beck. She knew with awful certainty that they shouldn't have given in to Uncle William's plans. But that was something she must keep to herself for the moment.

They had rooms on the first floor, comfortably furnished, with a shared bathroom. Auntie's room had a small table and easy chair arranged near a gas fire, a bookcase and a reading lamp by the bed. Franny's room was simply furnished—no fire, but a radiator in one corner, a narrow bed and an old-fashioned dressing table. It could have been a room in a small hotel—without colour, adequate and unwelcoming.

Mrs Beck went away. Hancock came with their luggage and Franny said, 'Will you ask someone to bring us some coffee, please? I think my aunt would have wished us to have some.'

Hancock looked surprised, muttered something and went away.

Auntie was sitting in the easy chair. She looked so forlorn that Franny gave her a hug and said cheerfully, 'I dare say Aunt Editha had to go out. You're rather tired; we were up so early.' She turned the gas fire on and waited until it glowed, then opened the first of her aunt's cases.

She was arranging her aunt's treasured photos and ornaments on the dressing table when a young girl came in with a tray on which were two cups of coffee and a small sugar bowl. She smiled in a friendly fashion and Franny thanked her and asked her name.

'Jenny, miss. The kitchenmaid. And there's Rose, the housemaid, and Mr Cox, the butler.'

When she had gone, Franny asked, 'Has the house changed, Auntie? It looks exactly as mother described it to me.'

Auntie looked around the room. 'The furniture is quite different. We had lovely antique furniture in our rooms—they were at the front of the house.' She added drily, 'This room, if I remember rightly, was our governess's.'

'Oh, I dare say they keep some of the rooms shut up nowadays,' said Franny. 'It must cost a lot to keep this place running.'

Auntie sipped her coffee. 'Your uncle inherited a good deal of money as well as this house and the title.'

Franny thought it was a good idea to change the subject. She went to look out of the window, remarking on the wintry gardens below. 'It will be nice for you to walk there later on,' she pointed out. 'I can't think why Aunt Editha didn't give you a room on the ground floor so that you could go in and out easily.' The idea of Auntie toiling up and down the stairs several times a day wasn't very satisfactory.

A gong summoned them to lunch and they went

downstairs and found Cox waiting in the hall, ready
to show them the way.

This annoyed Auntie, and she said quite snappily,
'There's no need to treat us as guests. I was born
and brought up here. I'm well aware of where the
dining room is.'

Aunt Editha was already sitting at the table. She
said, 'Forgive me if I don't get up. I'm exhausted
after a meeting of the parish council. You had a good
journey down, I hope? And you find your rooms
comfortable?'

For all the world as though they were unexpected
guests and not members of the family, thought
Franny indignantly. She settled Auntie in her chair
and sat down herself.

'We had a comfortable journey, Aunt Editha. Is it
not possible for Auntie to have a room on the ground
floor? The stairs are very tiring for her and a room
overlooking the garden would make it easier.' She
paused to look at the small portion of soup being
ladled in to her bowl. 'There's a room beside the
drawing room, isn't there? Mother told me about it.'

Aunt Editha turned to Auntie. 'If you are dissatisfied with your room you have only to say so.
William and I considered the room you have been
given to be entirely suitable.' She smiled thinly.
'Perhaps when the warm weather comes we may re-
consider Franny's suggestion. We have your welfare
very much at heart.'

Franny didn't believe a word of that, but she said

nothing more. She had been silly to broach the subject so soon after their arrival, but she'd thought that as family she could speak openly. Presently she asked, 'Where is Uncle William?'

'He found it necessary to go into Wimborne. You will see him at dinner this evening. I expect you would both like to rest this afternoon; tea is at half past four in the drawing room.'

Franny took Auntie back to her room presently, saw her onto her bed and well covered in a quilt, and then finished the unpacking before going to her own room to put away her own meagre wardrobe. That done, and Auntie peacefully asleep, she went downstairs wrapped in her old mac and let herself out of the house. There was no one about. A brisk walk in the grounds would cheer her up. Besides, she had a lot to think about. Their reception had been tepid. Aunt Editha had made it plain that they weren't particularly welcome, and the servants, with the exception of Jenny, were polite but unfriendly. She wondered what kind of a welcome they would get from Uncle William…

'I wish we hadn't come,' said Franny to a robin that was watching her from the hedge. 'It's a mistake. But what else could we do?'

Auntie needed care and attention, she, Franny, had no job, and there was almost no money. Uncle William had arrived just at a time when to ignore his plans for their future was an impossibility.

Franny, walking awkwardly because her ankle

hurt, decided that for the present, at least, they must make the best of it. Perhaps Uncle William would give them a warmer welcome than they had received from Aunt Editha.

Uncle William's welcome took the form of a speech in which he reminded them several times of his generosity in giving them a home, assuring them that they might spend the rest of their days there and that Auntie would be given every care and attention.

'And as for you, Francesca,' he finished in his overbearing way, 'I have no doubt that we shall find something to keep you happily occupied. I have already spoken to the rector—his curate, a very pleasant man, is in need of helpers for Sunday school and the Mother's Union.'

Franny held her tongue; Auntie was looking bewildered and unhappy and she didn't intend to add to her distress.

They dined presently. There was no need to make conversation for Uncle William did the talking. He shrugged aside anything Auntie had to say about Fish Street and embarked on a long description of the work which needed to be done on one wing of the house.

'An enormous expense!' he pointed out. 'But I must preserve our home at all costs. I have cut my pleasure to the bone in order to meet the cost,' he added sadly. 'And now the extra expense…'

'We didn't ask to come,' Franny pointed out

sharply. 'It is kind of you to give us a home, Uncle, but as soon as I am able to get work again Auntie and I will relieve you of the added burden on your finances.'

Uncle William went purple and choked, 'Francesca—I can only suppose that your rudeness is the result of undesirable friends.'

'I'm not meaning to be rude, just speaking the truth, Uncle. I should have thought that you and Aunt Editha would be glad to know that you won't have to keep us permanently.'

'I am shocked and so is your aunt. The ingratitude…'

'Well, you don't need to be shocked,' Franny pointed out reasonably. 'And of course we are grateful,' she added thoughtfully. 'Although I can't think why you didn't help us when Mother and Father were killed. You did nothing after their accident, only washed your hands of us.' She smiled at Auntie. 'We'd have sunk without trace if it hadn't been for Auntie.'

'I am appalled…' began Uncle William.

'So were we,' said Franny. 'I dare say you had your reasons,' she added kindly, 'but you did treat my mother and father very badly.' She paused because Auntie gave her such a distressed look. 'I've let my tongue run away with me,' she observed matter-of-factly. 'I always do. But at least it clears the air, doesn't it?'

Uncle William maintained a stony silence after

that, and it was left to Aunt Editha to make conversation with Auntie, ignoring Franny.

They would be tired, said Aunt Editha as they rose from the table. They would like to go to their rooms. Breakfast was at half past eight. She bade them goodnight, but Uncle William still didn't speak.

In Auntie's room, helping her to get ready for the night, Franny said, 'I shouldn't have spoken as I did; I'm sorry if it's bothered you. I never could hold my tongue. I dare say once they've got used to having us here it will be quite pleasant.'

She didn't believe that, of course, but Auntie needed a bit of cheering up. Once Auntie was in bed, Franny went to her own room and sat down to write to Finn. It was a cheerful letter and it took her quite a time to compose it. On no account must Finn doubt even for a moment that things weren't quite what they had expected. It's like being poor relations in a Victorian novel, thought Franny, and went to have a bath and reflect upon the day.

Her reflections did nothing to lift her spirits, so she gave them up and thought about the professor. Where was he? she wondered. And would she ever see him again? And, if she did, would he remember who she was? She rather doubted that. He would have hosts of friends, and when his work permitted she imagined that he would have a very pleasant social life.

The water grew cold at last, which put a stop to her fanciful thoughts, and she went to bed.

She woke in the night, knowing that a faint noise had roused her. She had left the doors open in the bathroom which separated her room from Auntie's and she got up now, wincing at the twinge of pain in her ankle, and padded across the cold bathroom floor—she heard the sound again. Auntie was crying.

Franny turned on the bedside light and sat down on the edge of the bed. 'It's only because you are tired,' she told her aunt. 'Everything will be all right in the morning. It wasn't quite what you expected, was it, dear? But I dare say Uncle William and Aunt Editha feel just as awkward as we do. We have to get to know each other, don't we, after all these years?'

Auntie said worriedly, 'I'm not sure that I trust your uncle, child. He was a vindictive young man. He never liked us, and certainly he had no affection for us. I wonder why he has sought us out in this unexpected fashion? It worries me.' And Auntie had reason to worry.

Over the years William had brooded over his young sisters' defiance until it had become an obsession. To make them pay had become vital to him. He had been thwarted by the death of Franny's mother, but had then merely transferred his hatred to her children.

It had been easy to keep track of his sister, Franny and Finn once he had had news of their mother and father's deaths, and that they were in straitened circumstances had been obvious from the Fish Street

address. He had bided his time. They were to be
coaxed to return to his home and once there he
would see to it that they paid for the disobedience
to him when his sisters had married.

Now everything had gone according to his plan.
Fate had been on his side.

His sister was ill, and as far as he was concerned
could die as soon as possible, and Francesca—as bad
or even worse than her mother had been—well, her
future was settled. He and Editha were getting old;
she should become their companion—unpaid, of
course—and dwindle away into a dreary spinster-
hood.

He was a rich man but mean; she wouldn't get a
penny piece…

Auntie, happily unaware of this, was still worried.
'And what about my pension…?'

Franny said soothingly, 'Don't worry about that,
Auntie. It will be all right, I'm sure.'

She began to talk about the things they would
do—walk in the village together, perhaps do some
shopping for Aunt Editha, potter in the garden, get
to know people—Aunt Editha must surely have
friends—there would be a game of bridge, perhaps,
and television to watch.

Auntie allowed herself to be soothed, but said
worriedly, 'Yes, dear, that's all very well, but what
about you? You need to meet people of your age,
lead your own life. You can't spend your days just

sitting around with old women playing bridge and knitting.'

'Don't worry about me; I'm sure Uncle William will find me something to do.' Franny kissed Auntie's cheek. 'Now go to sleep, my dear; everything is going to be all right.'

Only it wasn't. It took a day or so for Franny to realise that they really were to be treated like the poor relations.

Auntie was expected to spend a good deal of the day in her room—after all she had been gravely ill. 'It is most important that you rest quietly,' Uncle William had said. 'Come downstairs to meals, by all means, but I suggest you remain in your room for the greater part of the day.'

Franny had protested at that. 'Auntie needs to have gentle exercise,' she'd pointed out. 'If you could arrange for her to have a room downstairs so that she could go into the garden without having to go up and down the stairs? And could you get your doctor to come and just check that she is well?'

'Quite unnecessary...'

'Then I'll have to go and find him for myself.'

'Certainly not. I will attend to it. It is obvious that you have nothing better to do than find fault with the arrangements which have been made for you both. You are more like your father than your mother, I regret to say.'

'Don't you dare speak of my father in that manner. He was worth half a dozen of you, Uncle William!'

He had walked out of the room then, and although he'd been polite enough when they sat down to lunch later she'd sensed his displeasure. She had dared to remind him about the doctor and wanting the rooms changed, and she had been abominably rude. He wouldn't forgive her in a hurry.

Two days later Rose the housemaid went on holiday, and Aunt Editha suggested that Franny might help with one or two small chores around the house. 'I'm sure you will be glad to have something to do,' she pointed out. 'Just small jobs around the place— the flowers, laying the table, and little errands for Mrs Beck…'

It didn't stop at 'little errands', however. She did the flowers and then within a few days Franny found herself answering the door when Cox was in the cellars or had an afternoon off, making beds because Mrs Beck needed Jenny to help her in the kitchen, loading the washing machine, hanging the wash to dry in one of the outhouses bordering the yard at the back and, since there seemed no one else to do it, ironing it.

'When is Rose coming back?' she asked her aunt as she cleared the breakfast table one morning.

'I have had a letter from her. Her mother is poorly; she won't be returning for some time, I'm afraid. Fortunately you are here, so there is no need for me to engage help until she returns.'

'I am your niece, Aunt Editha, not the housemaid.'

'I must remind you, Francesca, that you and your

aunt are here owing to the kindness and generosity of your uncle. If you are dissatisfied then go, by all means, and take your aunt with you.'

'You mean that?'

'Certainly.'

They had nowhere to go and almost no money. No house, no furniture and no friends. And it was February and cold. On her own, Franny would have walked out of the house as fast as she could pack her bags, but Auntie needed warmth and food and a bed to sleep in. She had no choice but to stay.

She said nothing to Auntie. There was a half-formed plan in her head, though. Auntie was due for another check-up in a week or so. She would go with her, explain matters to the doctor who saw her and ask if she could be given a bed in a long-stay hospital. That would leave Franny free to find work and somewhere to live, and as quickly as possible have Auntie back with her. It was a plan full of holes, but the best she could think of at the moment.

Cautiously she sounded out Auntie the next day, whilst sitting with her for an hour after lunch. 'You're due to go back to St Giles' in just over a week. I'm not sure how we shall get there, but I should think Uncle William will let us have the car. Auntie, have you any money? Has your pension been paid? Were they going to send it to you here?'

'William saw to it for me. He told me that I must sign a paper allowing him to deal with it.'

'And you did sign?'

'Well, yes, dear. You know how forceful your uncle is. He said something about opening an account…'

She looked so worried that Franny said quickly, 'What a good idea. I'm sure he'll remember to let you have it. I must go; it's almost tea time.'

'I don't see you very much,' said Auntie. 'I do hope you are getting out a bit and meeting people.'

'Once the weather gets better, we'll go out in the garden,' promised Franny. 'The housemaid has had to stay home for a few more days, so I do the flowers and make the beds to help out. But I'm coming to have tea with you in a little while.'

Auntie looked worried. 'I'm sure William means to be kind, but he is so strict. I have no wish to spend the rest of my days cooped up here in this room, and as for you, Franny, I believe you are being made use of. If only I could talk to William or Editha, but I see them so seldom, and then only for a few minutes. Of course, Editha has a busy life with her committees and charities and the church…'

Franny replied suitably; Auntie was slow to think ill of anyone and to keep her content was important. But she would have to ask Uncle William about Auntie's check-up at St Giles', and she would ask yet again if her aunt might have a room on the ground floor.

Auntie had always been a busy, bustling person, and even though she hadn't liked living in Fish Street she had cheerfully made the best of it. But it seemed to Franny that now she had become listless and apathetic, ripe ground for Uncle William's overbearing ways. A dozen times a day Franny told herself that something must be done, and a dozen times a day she longed for the professor who would know what to do and do it.

While making tea for the ladies who had come to play bridge with Aunt Editha, Franny wondered where he was and what he was doing…

He was in Sister's office at his out-patients clinic, looking through the patients' notes for the following week. He had been back from Belgium for quite a while, working long hours, but now at least he could take things more easily. And since Auntie was due for a check-up, he would see Franny again soon.

He went through the notes with his usual care and then he turned to Sister, who was sitting at the other side of the desk.

'I don't see Mrs Blake's notes—she's due in next week, is she not?'

Sister looked surprised. 'You haven't been told? We had a phone call saying that she was leaving London and would be in the care of another doctor. It was a man who called; he said he was family and said he would give us an address and the doctor's name so that we could forward her notes and send a letter to the doctor. We've not heard a word since.'

She saw his quick frown. 'We wanted to telephone

to Fish Street but they're not on the phone, and the three letters we have sent haven't been answered.'

'You have no idea where Mrs Blake might be?'

'Absolutely none, sir.'

'She had a niece working at a nursing home in Pimlico—The Haven…'

He picked up the phone, asked for the home's number and presently dialled. Miss Bowen no longer worked there, he was told. She had sprained her ankle and there had been no question of her job being kept open for her. He put down the phone, wished Sister a pleasant good afternoon, went to his car and drove to Fish Street.

How like Franny to do something silly like spraining her ankle, he thought angrily. And where was she? Unlikely to be at Fish Street, but the neighbours might know.

The house was empty and forlorn and there was no one in either of the neighbouring houses. He got back into his car and picked up the phone.

Finn was in his room studying. His three room-mates were getting ready to go out for a meal, but he had a paper to finish. Besides, he couldn't afford it. They got on well together, and he wasn't surprised when Josh banged on his door, no doubt trying to tempt him to join them.

'Go away, Josh, I must get this finished before I go to bed. I'll boil an egg later. Have a good time…'

The door opened and he turned round. The professor strolled in, nodded to Josh, and then shut the door behind him.

Finn got to his feet. 'Professor—sir—how did you know where I was?'

The professor smiled. 'I made a few enquiries. Tell me, where are your aunt and sister and why are you not at Fish Street?'

Finn cleared some books off the one easy chair. 'It's quite a long story, sir!'

The professor made himself comfortable. 'I have all evening,' he observed mildly. 'Don't leave anything out. I'm anxious about your aunt...'

'But Uncle William said—'

'Begin at the beginning, Finn.'

'Well,' said Finn. 'Franny sprained her ankle quite badly, and Auntie wasn't well...'

He began to talk and the professor didn't interrupt. Only when Finn fell silent did he say, 'Do you suppose they're happy with your uncle?'

'No. I don't think so. Franny writes to me once a week, but her letters don't say anything, if you know what I mean, and they're so cheerful. I mean, she's a cheerful girl, but she writes as though someone's looking over her shoulder.'

The professor got out of his chair. 'I think that something must be done about that. Come back with me now—never mind that—' he nodded at the sheets of paper on the table '—I'll put in a word. We will have a meal and see what is to be done.'

Finn, always hungry, brightened. 'I say, sir, really?'

'Really. Better leave a note for your friends.'

'I'm not very tidy,' Finn pointed out.

'You'll do. Come along.'

They drove to Wimpole Street and the professor ushered Finn into his elegant hall to be met by Crisp, who, taking Finn in his stride, wished them good evening.

'Evening, Crisp. Finn, Crisp runs this place for me. Mr Bowen is a medical student, Crisp.'

'A noble profession, sir,' said Crisp. 'Do you care to dine at once?'

'Ten minutes, Crisp; we're both famished.'

The professor's large hand propelled Finn across the hall and into a room overlooking the street. 'Sit down; there's time for us to have a drink. I've rather a nice dry sherry…'

Finn sat and looked around him. The drawing room, he supposed, seeing the large high-ceilinged room, with its panelled walls and a highly polished floor partly covered by a thin silky carpet. It looked old, but he decided that it might be valuable. The furniture was a nice mixture of comfortable chairs and some beautiful antique pieces, and there was a bowl of tulips on the rent table under the window. There was a brisk fire in a rather splendid marble fireplace, in front of which Trimble the cat dozed.

The sight of him somehow put Finn at his ease, and by the time they sat down to dine in an equally beautiful room he had quite lost his awe of the professor and made a hearty meal of game soup, lamb chops with a variety of vegetables, and an apple tart with cream.

'Does Crisp do the cooking?' he asked.

'Yes, he's excellent, isn't he? Shall we have coffee in the drawing room? I have one or two ideas to discuss with you.' When they were sitting once more by the fire the professor spoke.

'Listen carefully, this is what we shall do…'

CHAPTER SIX

FRANNY was worried, and puzzled, too. There had been no letter from St Giles' reminding Auntie of her appointment, and when she'd told her uncle this, and asked if she might phone the hospital, he had told her coldly that he would do so himself. He wrote down the phone number and assured her that he would attend to the matter, before picking up his newspaper again.

'And the local doctor,' persisted Franny. 'Auntie isn't as well as she should be.'

'You are being unnecessarily fussy, Francesca. I have told our doctor that your aunt is living here and given him some idea of her operation. He will call if he thinks it necessary.'

Franny persisted. 'But it is necessary. It is very important that for the next few months she is under a doctor's care. Did you give him our doctor's letter about Auntie?'

Uncle William lowered the newspaper and glared at her. 'I find your lack of trust in me quite beyond comprehension. Stop this silly interfering and go and make yourself useful to your aunt.'

'I'm not fussing,' said Franny. 'And I'm already being useful, doing Rose's work. Tell me, uncle, do you expect me to go on doing the housemaid's work—unpaid, of course?'

He answered harshly, 'Yes, Francesca, I do, in return for the care and attention my sister is receiving. Did you think that you would be treated as a daughter of the house? New clothes, pocket money, a social life?' He laughed nastily. 'It will be my sister who suffers if you try and alter my plans.'

She wasn't puzzled any more, only her worry had increased.

Going to the village to shop for the housekeeper, she used some of Aunty's scanty money to phone Finn. There was no answer. She got her money back and tried the hospital. She had to wait for a reply, and then there was a delay while she was put through to the cardiac department. She waited again until a voice asked her what she wanted. At the same time she was cut off. She had no more money.

It was wretched weather, a cold rain and a nasty wind, but she didn't notice that as she walked back to the house with her shopping. She gulped back tears of frustration and tried to think what to do.

Uncle William had made it very plain that, in return for giving them a home, he expected something, and since Auntie's health was what mattered Franny had no choice but to take up the role she had been given—a job which seemed to cover almost everything from washing to making a fourth at bridge. She would have to dance to his tune for the moment, but she would write to the hospital and do her best to discover why Auntie had had no letter to attend the clinic. And somehow or other—she didn't quite know how—she would go and see Uncle William's doctor and explain about Auntie.

The next morning she was up early. Mrs Beck, Aunt Editha had told her, was to have a few days off. 'I'm sure you won't mind getting breakfast for us, Francesca. Your uncle likes eggs and bacon and a few mushrooms, but I'll have scrambled eggs. At half past eight.'

Aunt had slept badly, so Franny brought her a cup of tea and the promise of a light breakfast and sped back to the kitchen. Cox was already there, expecting his own meal, grumbling to Jenny as she made the toast.

'The place is at sixes and sevens since you came, miss,' he told Franny. He cast an eye over the dish of bacon and eggs she was arranging on a tray.

'The master likes his bacon very crisp—I doubt he'll eat that…'

'Then he can come and cook it for himself,' said Franny. 'I'll have my breakfast here, if you don't mind; it'll save time.'

She sent Jenny upstairs with a tray for Auntie, cooked more bacon for Cox, then sat down to drink her tea and eat a slice of toast. Since Mrs Beck wasn't there, she suspected that she would be expected to cook lunch, as well as dinner that evening. If only she could get out of the house for an hour or so she could go to the village and discover where the doctor lived.

Cox came back presently. 'The master wouldn't eat his bacon,' he told her with gloomy triumph. 'He wants you in the dining room, miss.'

Franny finished her tea. Swathed in one of Mrs Beck's aprons, her hair in an untidy pile on top of her head, and with no make-up on, she left the kitchen and went into the hall through the green baize door, just as the doorbell rang.

It was probably the postman with something too large to go through the letter box. She opened the door.

The professor, closely followed by Finn, walked past her into the hall.

Franny closed the door and stood looking at them. She had gone very pale and hadn't uttered a word. If it wasn't a miracle, it was a very nice dream.

It was Finn who spoke. 'Hello, Franny. You look a bit under the weather...'

The professor hadn't spoken. He stood looking at Franny, reflecting that each time he saw her she hardly looked her best. Indeed, she looked fit to drop. He was aware of a fierce rage that she should look like that, but his voice was quiet when he did speak at last.

'It took a little while to discover where you were. Can we go somewhere and talk?'

She shook her head. 'Uncle William will have heard the doorbell and will want to know who it is.'

She managed a smile. 'I'm so glad you've come. I'm worried about Auntie…'

'Why are you in an apron?'

'The cook's on holiday.'

'You look like a servant,' said Finn indignantly.

'Well, I am. If I don't help in the house, I…Auntie will suffer for it.'

'I should like a word with your uncle. What is his name?'

'Sir William Meredith. He's just finishing breakfast.'

'Then let us take his appetite away,' said the professor, in such a savage voice that Franny took a step backwards.

They were crossing the hall when the dining room door was thrust open and Uncle William came out. 'Who is at the door?' he bellowed. 'Come here, Francesca.'

He stopped short when he saw the professor and Finn.

'Is this your brother? What is he doing here? He need not think that he can live off me, too.'

'No fear of that,' said Finn. 'Uncle William, this is Professor van der Kettener.'

Uncle William opened his mouth to speak, but he was given no chance.

'I will do the talking, Sir William. I understand that you have deliberately withheld information concerning my patient, Mrs Blake. She is in my care and should be checked either by myself or her doctor. I'm informed that you undertook to give St Giles' all the information needed when you took Mrs Blake into your care. Moreover, she has given up her home under the impression that you would make her welcome and care for her. Presumably you offered Francesca a home as well.'

His voice was cold and the eyes he turned on Franny were icy. 'From the look of her, you have used her as a kitchenmaid. I propose to take Mrs Blake back with me now, and, of course, Francesca will leave, too.'

'You can't do that,' Uncle William blustered.

'No? Tell me, have you contacted your doctor concerning Mrs Blake since she arrived here? Have you tried to contact the hospital?'

'There has been no need. My sister is perfectly well...'

'That's a lie,' said Franny. 'I've asked you time and again to get the doctor or ring St Giles'. I would like,' said Franny strongly, 'to throw something at you—you're a tyrant.'

The professor's mouth twitched. 'Take Finn with you, Franny,' he said mildly. 'Get Auntie warmly wrapped up—don't bother to dress her if she is still in bed—and pack your things. And—er—tidy yourself.'

He turned to look at Sir William, who was gobbling with rage. 'Perhaps we might go somewhere and have a talk?' he said pleasantly. 'This is quite a serious matter, you know.'

'Take my sister if you want to. But Francesca is to stay here. She is my niece; you have no right to take her away.'

'Oh, but I have. You see, we are to be married.'

Franny, about to mount the stairs, gave a gasp and would have turned round, but Finn gave her a shove and hissed, 'Be quiet, leave it to the professor.'

She was propelled upstairs and into Auntie's room. 'He didn't mean it?' whispered Franny.

Finn shrugged. 'How should I know? Uncle William can't do a thing if the professor says you are to be married. First I've heard of it.'

There was no chance to say more. Auntie—surprised into tears—had to be told and reassured, got out of bed, wrapped in her dressing gown, her coat and a shawl or two and then sat in a chair while Franny packed her bags. That done, she left Finn with Auntie and went towards her own room, first going onto the landing to try and see what was happening.

It was quiet in the hall below. She could hear the murmur of voices from her uncle's study, and then her aunt came out of the dining room, calling for Cox. Franny went to her room then and packed in a haphazard fashion, afraid that if she wasn't ready the professor would go without her. Then she spent a very necessary ten minutes doing her face and brushing her hair into a neat topknot before getting her coat and going back to Auntie's room.

The professor was there, with Aunt Editha, bending over Auntie, talking to her in a voice calculated to soothe the most timid of patients.

He straightened up, saw Franny and smiled at her. 'Ready? Good girl. Finn, bring the bags; I'll carry Mrs Blake down to the car.' He added smoothly, 'I dare say you want to say goodbye to your aunt and uncle, Franny.'

'Yes,' said Franny. 'I want to say goodbye and that I hope never to see them again.'

'You ungrateful girl.' Aunt Editha's voice shook with rage. 'After all that we've done for you. I'm glad you're going. I want nothing more to do with you—either of you.'

'Oh, good,' said Franny, and went downstairs behind Finn. Cox was in the hall, trying to look as though he wasn't dying of curiosity. He opened the door for the professor, and Finn went ahead to open the car door while Franny crossed the hall to the study.

Her uncle was there, standing with his back to the fire, smoking a cigar.

'Goodbye, uncle.' She didn't give him time to reply, but closed the door gently and went out to the car.

'Get in front,' said the professor. 'Finn will sit with Auntie and support her.'

'Wouldn't it be better…?' began Franny as he got in and drove away.

'No. I want you to tell me exactly what happened, Franny.'

If he had sounded in the least bit sympathetic or turned to smile at her, she would have burst into tears, letting loose the flood of unhappiness and worry she had fought over the last week or so. But he was looking ahead and his voice had been matter-of-fact.

She swallowed resentment and told him exactly what had been happening. She managed to be as matter-of-fact as he had sounded and she didn't look at him. When she had told him the whole sorry story, she thanked him politely for going to so much trouble in looking for them. 'We can never repay you,' she told him, 'but we are truly grateful.'

He grunted something and then said, 'I'm going to stop at the next service station. We could all do with coffee. Then I'm taking Auntie straight to St Giles'. I want her thoroughly checked. She needs proper rest and an opportunity to get reorganised.'

He had nothing more to say then, only asking Finn over his shoulder if Auntie was comfortable. And presently, when he pulled in at a service station, he made no bones about carrying Auntie through the entrance and setting her gently down outside the Ladies.

'I'll be here,' he told Franny. 'Finn will get the coffee and have it ready for us.'

He put out a hand and touched Franny's cheek with a gentle finger. His touch brought tears to her eyes, but she sniffed them back.

'Don't cry now, my dear! We'll talk later and then you may cry all you want.'

She sniffed again and nodded, staring up into his calm face. Then she put an arm around Auntie and led her away.

Between them they walked Auntie to the café and sat her down at the table Finn had found. There was coffee and sandwiches. Finn, making great inroads into them, said cheerfully, 'We left town at six o'clock—breakfast seems ages ago.' He glanced at the professor. 'I suppose you'll tell Franny all about it later, sir?'

'Yes, all in good time. You'll want to talk to your sister, too. When we've settled Auntie comfortably, we'll go home and have a meal, then you had better go back to your studies, Finn.'

'OK sir.' He added awkwardly, 'You've been no end of a help. Thank you for that. I can never repay you, only by working hard and succeeding.'

He had gone very red, but Franny gave him a warm smile and the professor put out a large hand. 'Shake on our success, Finn. I could never have succeeded without you.'

They didn't sit there for long. Auntie was perfectly happy, but the sudden excitement had made her drowsy. Back in the car once more, they drove on, hardly speaking, although the silence was a contented one. As they neared St Giles' the professor picked up his phone and requested a stretcher to be waiting for them. And, sure enough, when he drew to a gentle stop before one casualty entrance, there was his registrar and a nurse beside the porters.

He must be very important, thought Franny, and wondered what was to happen next.

She waited with Finn while Auntie was laid on the stretcher, and wished her goodbye for the moment.

'I'll be in to see you very soon,' said Franny, not knowing how that could be brought about. Perhaps she could stay with Finn for a day or two while she looked for a job.

The professor left his patient for a moment. 'Finn, get a taxi and both of you go to Wimpole Street. I'll be with you as soon as I can. Crisp is expecting you.' He slipped some notes into Finn's hand. 'Make yourselves comfortable.'

In the taxi, Franny asked. 'Where are we going? And who is Crisp?'

'The professor's man. He's got a flat over his rooms at Wimpole Street. I went there last night and had dinner with him while he cooked up this plan to get you away from Uncle William. Was it bad, Franny?'

'Yes. And, you see, we hadn't any money. I'll tell you about it later. I've told the professor.' She peered out of the window. 'Are we nearly there? It looks nice…'

Crisp welcomed them in a fatherly fashion when they arrived. 'Miss Bowen would like to freshen up? The cloakroom is just here.' He opened a door at the back of the hall and she retired thankfully, delighted to see that there was everything there that a woman could possibly need—make-up, brushes, combs, toilet water—a choice of bottles, too—a pile of towels, soaps, even several toothbrushes in their cellophane packs arranged beside a choice of toothpastes.

A kind of cosmetic heaven, thought Franny, taking the pins out of her hair.

Ten minutes later she joined Finn in the drawing room. She still looked far from her best, but even Finn, as unobservant as most brothers, noticed that she looked more like herself.

The professor, joining them some half an hour later, was of the same opinion as Finn although he didn't say so. Franny was too thin, too pale and too tired, but there was the light of battle in the eyes she turned on him. He guessed that she had thought up several arguments as to her future and Auntie's. She was so independent, and as prickly as a hedgehog if she suspected that she was receiving favours.

'May we talk?' she asked him.

'Certainly. But may we have a meal first? Finn is starving, and so am I, and I dare say you are, too.'

She went red. 'I beg your pardon. I didn't mean to be rude. It's just that there's such a lot to sort out. And we've caused you sufficient bother already. I'll go back with Finn.'

'No, you won't,' said Finn forcefully, and the professor laughed.

'Let us have lunch and I'll tell you about Auntie.'

Crisp had performed miracles in his kitchen. There was soup—delicious and home-made—followed by a mouthwatering steak and kidney pie, creamed potatoes and several vegetables, and lastly queen of puddings, washed down by lager for the men and red wine for Franny. They had their coffee at the table while the professor told them about Auntie.

'I'd like to keep her at St Giles' for a week.' He saw Franny's startled look. 'No, she isn't ill, only run-down through lack of proper exercise and the right food. She will go to physiotherapy each day and have gentle exercises. All that sitting around in one room did her no good at all. She told me that you had tried to have her room changed to one on the ground floor, but that your uncle wouldn't agree. Nor would he agree to a doctor, would he? A petty tyrant to his family.'

'He can't make us go back, can he?' asked Franny.

'No. He might try to bully you into returning, but I don't think that he will.' He smiled a little. 'Let us go into the drawing room by the fire.'

'I must get a job as far away as possible, where Auntie will be quite safe,' said Franny. 'I'll start looking for something tomorrow morning.'

'You will not need to do that. Auntie will come here, Franny.'

'Here? What do you mean? And, of course, I must get a job…'

'She will live here with us, and when we go to Holland I will find someone to keep her company.'

'When we go to Holland?' Franny's voice came out in a startled squeak. 'But I'm not going to Holland.'

'I rather hoped that as my wife you would like to go with me.'

'Your wife?' She threw him a look of amazement.

'Well, yes. You heard me telling your uncle that we were to be married?'

'Yes, but that was to stop him trying to make me stay at Brinsleigh.'

'Of course it was…'

'You didn't mean it.'

'You realise that your uncle will be certain to check on it? If he finds that it was nothing but a hollow statement by me, he will make it his business to trace you and Auntie. He may not be able to make you return, but he could make life very unpleasant. And unpleasantness is something Auntie must be spared.'

He spoke with quiet assurance, and Franny, a variety of feelings churning up her insides, was in no state to find holes in his calm assessment of the situation. He smiled at her now and got up. 'I'll take Finn back now; we will talk again when I return.'

Finn was already on his feet. He liked the idea of the professor for a brother-in-law and he rather thought that he would make Franny a good husband. He hoped that Franny wasn't going to be pig-headed about it. Of course, it must have been a bit of a surprise, but it would be a marvellous solution for their futures. He was surprised that the professor wanted to marry Franny, though. She was a splendid sister, who had taken enough knocks to upset any girl, but she was nothing much to look at.

He said now, 'Thank you for lunch, it was first rate. Franny, let me know what's going to happen. I'll phone the hospital about Auntie in the morning.'

He patted her awkwardly on the shoulder. 'Bit of a turn-up, wasn't it?'

'Yes,' said Franny. 'I was so very glad to see you—you both—I can't quite believe it. I'll let you know where I'll be as soon as I know.'

In the car presently, Finn asked diffidently, 'You really want to marry Franny, sir?'

'Yes, Finn. A medical man needs a wife, you know.' He spoke kindly, but Finn heard the reserve in his voice and didn't ask any more questions.

As for Franny, she sat by the fire with Trimble on her knee, her head in a fine muddle. All this talk of getting married was nonsense, of course, but at the same time the professor wasn't a man to talk nonsense. Surely it wasn't necessary to marry her in order to get her away from Uncle William?

'I don't know anything about him,' she told Trimble. 'The whole idea is crazy.'

Trimble muttered and twitched his whiskers, which hardly helped.

It was dusk before the professor returned, closely followed by Crisp with the tea tray. He settled himself in his chair and begged Franny to pour the tea.

The teapot was Georgian silver and the cups and saucers Coalport china. She poured carefully, terrified of breaking something, trying to think of something to say.

The professor handed her a plate of wafer-thin sandwiches. 'I can see that you're bursting with questions. Do ask them when you want to, only don't be too long about it—I have to return to the hospital shortly and my secretary is coming this evening. She will keep you company.' He added, in a matter-of-fact voice, 'She will spend the night here too.'

'Why?'

'I have some old-fashioned ideas, Franny. One of them is that you don't sleep under my roof without another woman in the house.'

'Your reputation...?'

'No, no. Yours.' He caught her eye. 'And don't argue about it, Franny.'

'No, well, I won't. Not now at least. You keep talking as though we're to marry. I can quite see that it was a good idea to tell Uncle William that, but you didn't mean it, did you?'

'Indeed, I did.' He passed her a plate of little cakes. 'Use your wits, Franny. Your uncle is no fool. He might not be able to claim the right to keep Auntie at his home, for he has no legal grounds for that, but there is the faint possibility that he could interfere in your life. I know you are over twenty-one and independent, but he could argue that as a close relation he has the right to give you a home since you are homeless and without work.'

'You won't let him…?' began Franny. 'Anyway, I'd run away.'

'No need to do that. I'll get a special licence and we will marry as soon as it can be arranged. He'll be unable to touch you once you are my wife.'

'That's all very well, but do you want a wife? Especially me…'

'As I told Finn, a medical man needs a wife. I have never had the time to fall in love or find the woman I want for my wife. I'm no longer a youth and it seems that this is unlikely now. I believe that we will suit each other quite well and I promise you that I won't rush you. We hardly know each other, but that is something that we can put right after we are married.'

He sounded placid, quite sure of himself, and entirely without sentiment. He passed his cup for more tea, entirely at his ease, smiling a little.

If this was a proposal of marriage, thought Franny, it must surely be unique. 'I'd like to think about it,' she said finally. 'I'm not sure if I'm the right wife for you.' She looked at him steadily. 'I'm rather plain, you know, and Fish Street is very different from this.' She waved a hand at their elegant surroundings.

'I fancy that you are more at home here than you were in Fish Street. And, as for your looks, I have never wished to marry a ravishing beauty—too distracting!'

Which wasn't quite the answer a girl would have expected from the man who had asked her to marry him. Still, it was better than nothing and, since it was evident that sentimental feelings of any sort were not to be evident either, it was what she should have expected.

'It is very kind of you,' she began inadequately, 'but I really can't marry you. You've forgotten Auntie…'

'I have forgotten nothing. I have already said that Auntie shall stay here until such time as she wishes to make a home for herself again. I rather think that she will wish to do that, and I know just the right woman to act as her housekeeper.'

Franny eyed him thoughtfully. 'You have thought of everything…'

The thought flashed through her mind that supposing he or she should fall in love? Had he thought of that? She voiced that thought.

'We might fall in love—I don't mean you and me, but with someone else.'

He answered her seriously, but she had the feeling that he was amused about something. 'Then we must be sure to tell each other, mustn't we?'

He glanced at his watch. 'I must go. I shall bring Mrs Willett back with me. She is a widow, and a very pleasant person. I hope that you will like her.' He got up and went to the door. 'Crisp will show

you to your room; you will want to unpack. I hope
we will be back before eight o'clock. Phone the hospital if you're anxious about Auntie.'

He went away quietly and she sat there, thinking
about the future he was offering her. She could quite
see that she wasn't going to alter his life; his work
was all-important to him, and taking a wife was
something which he considered he should do. He
would be a kind and considerate husband—she had
no doubt of that—just as long as she didn't make
any demands upon him. And since he had decided
that he should marry, she might just as well be his
wife as anyone else. A businesslike arrangement
with the warmth of a liking for each other which
might in the course of time turn into something
deeper. And Auntie would be safe and cared for...

Crisp came to interrupt her thoughts. He led her
across the hall and along a short passage, and opened
a door at its end. The room was a fair size, with a
window overlooking a narrow garden. It was warm
and softly lit by pink-shaded lamps, and furnished
charmingly with a walnut bed and dressing table,
two small easy chairs covered in rose-patterned cretonne and a tallboy inlaid with marquetry. The curtains were of the same cretonne and the quilt which
covered the bed was pink.

Crisp indicated her luggage. 'You will wish to unpack, Miss Bowen. The bathroom is through this
door. If I can be of help in any way, please ask.'

She peered into the bathroom—cream tiles, fluffy

pink towels, a shelf full of soaps and creams, lotions and powders. A room used by a woman, thought Franny. She must ask the professor if he had a mother or sisters…

She dawdled over her unpacking, did her hair and her face, decided that there wasn't much point changing into the one decent dress she possessed, and went back to the drawing room.

A little while later the professor came home with Mrs Willett, a cosy, middle-aged lady with a friendly face and a soft voice who was presently led away to her room by Crisp with a warning that dinner would be in half an hour.

The professor gave Franny a drink, poured one for himself, and sat down. 'I've seen Auntie again,' he told her. 'She is perfectly happy and her general condition is good. I'll keep her there for a few days while they get her going on some gentle exercise. She sends her love.'

He talked of this and that, then, putting her at her ease, so that by the time Mrs Willett joined them Franny, soothed by his quiet voice and warmed by the sherry, felt quite her old self.

After dinner the professor went to his study and she and Mrs Willett sat by the fire, talking. Mrs Willett had a daughter the same age as Franny, married and living in the north of England, and presently Franny found that she was telling her about herself and Finn and Auntie. Mrs Willett, primed by the professor, already knew the bare bones of it, but she

bent a kind and sympathetic ear now, and when
Franny had finished she spoke with real sympathy.

'You've had a miserable time, my dear, but now
you can look forward to a happy future. Professor
van der Kettener tells me that you are to be married.
He will be a kind and good husband; you can depend
upon that. I have worked for him for several years
when he has been here in England, and you couldn't
wish for a better man.'

He joined them presently, and after a short time
he suggested that Franny might like to go to bed.
'You must be tired,' he told her, 'and after all the
excitement you need a rest. Crisp will call you in
the morning. I'll see you at breakfast.'

So Franny bade Mrs Willett goodnight, and when
the professor opened the door for her she paused to
wish him goodnight, too. 'I hope you sleep well too,'
she told him.

The professor, satisfied that his plans had been
successful, assured her that he would.

Her room looked inviting. She had a long, hot
bath, then climbed into bed and found that someone
had put a glass of warm milk on the bedside table.
She drank it down, wondering sleepily why it tasted
so delicious, not knowing that it was discreetly laced
with the best brandy, so making doubly sure that she
had a good night's sleep.

The three of them breakfasted together in the morning, but presently Mrs Willett went back to her room

and the professor put his letters down.

'Crisp will take you to St Giles' when you wish,' he told Franny. 'And would it be a good idea if you did some shopping afterwards?' He caught her look. 'Yes, I know you haven't any money. I've an account at Harrods, so go there and buy whatever you want. I'll let them know.' He smiled suddenly. 'You will need a wedding dress for a start…'

'Oh, well, yes. I suppose I will. What else should I buy? I don't want you to be ashamed of me.' Franny was trying to match his matter-of-fact manner. 'I could get everything except the dress at Marks and Spencer.'

He said easily, 'Oh, you don't need to be too economical; get everything at Harrods. If I give you an idea of how much you can spend that would make it easier, wouldn't it?'

And when she nodded he named a sum which left her open-mouthed. 'That's too much. I couldn't possibly…'

He said smoothly, 'I think that just for once we might be a little extravagant, don't you, Franny?'

'Well,' said Franny, 'it would be lovely to buy clothes without looking at the price tag first. It will only be us at our wedding?'

'Er, yes. And your aunt and Finn, of course.'

She nodded. 'In a church…?'

'Of course. I'll see about the licence today.' He

gathered up his letters, preparing to go. 'Have you any preference as to the day?'

'No. Whenever it fits in with your work.' Franny frowned. 'You know, I'm still not sure that I'm the right wife for you. I know it's only a friendly arrangement—I mean, we aren't—that is, we don't love each other—but I don't know anything about you.'

'But you like me a little now, and you trust me?'

'Yes. I didn't like you very much at first, you know, but now I do, and of course I trust you. You've gone to a lot of trouble, too.'

'Then leave everything to me, Franny.' He went to the door, stooping to kiss her cheek lightly as he went. 'I shall be home about five o'clock, but I must go out again this evening.'

He put a small roll of notes by her plate and had gone before she could thank him.

Mrs Willett was in the hall when Franny entered it presently. 'I'll be back this evening, Franny. Have a lovely day shopping. I hope you'll show me everything.'

Franny sat down at the table again and presently Crisp came to clear it. 'You will want to go to the hospital later, Miss Bowen? I'll drive you there, and I was to remind you to take a taxi to Harrods from the hospital when you are ready to leave.'

It was a pleasant feeing, she reflected, being so carefully looked after. After years of penny-pinching and worrying about making ends meet, to be given carte blanche at Harrods was like a dream. But then the whole of the last day had been a dream. No one would believe it if I told them, thought Franny.

She went in search of Crisp and asked if he would take her to the hospital in half an hour. It was still early, but she realised with rising delight that she had a lot of shopping to do.

CHAPTER SEVEN

AUNTIE was up and dressed, waiting to go to Physiotherapy. 'I am so comfortable here,' she told Franny happily. 'Tomorrow I'm to start doing exercises. Marc came to see me just now; he says I'll be as good as new in a short time. My dear, he says I am to stay at his home until I decide to make a home for myself and Finn. And you are to be married. I could scarcely believe it.'

'Nor can I,' said Franny. 'I'm going shopping. The prof—that is, Marc—says I must have some new clothes.' She smiled widely. 'Harrods.'

'Only what you deserve, love. Do you suppose we shall hear from William again?'

'If we do, we only have to tell Marc,' said Franny largely. 'He'll know what to do. So don't worry, dear. Did Finn phone?'

'Yes. I was to tell you that everything is fine. He will ring you this evening. Oh, my dear, can you imagine how wonderful it would be if I could have a home of my own again? With Finn popping in and out and you close by? It's like a dream!' She gave Franny a thoughtful look. 'You'll be happy with Marc? It's all so sudden; I had no idea that he was in love with you.'

Franny stopped herself just in time from saying that she'd had no idea either. Let Auntie enjoy her romantic thoughts.

Obedient to her instructions, Franny took a taxi to Harrods, over-tipped the cabby for the sheer pleasure of it and entered the elegant doors. She looked a little out of place among the stylish customers wandering around as she made her way to the dress department. She explored it for some time, aware of the sharp eyes of the sales ladies, before going up to one of them.

'My name is Bowen, Miss Francesca Bowen. Professor van der Kettener has an account here and has told me to charge anything I buy to him. Would you verify this before I start shopping?'

The sales lady looked surprised, begged her to be seated while she did as she was asked, and went away. How awful, thought Franny, if he has forgotten.

She should have known better; he never forgot. A smiling lady returned and, despite the heavy make-up and strange hairstyle, turned out to be both friendly and helpful.

'Are you looking for just an outfit or a complete wardrobe?' she asked. She thought Franny was a plain girl, shabbily dressed, but it would be a pleasure to dress her...

'I want something for a quiet wedding—something I can wear afterwards. A dress and matching coat? I shall need some shoes and gloves and a handbag and a hat. I would also like something to wear every day—a jersey dress, perhaps, skirts and blouses and one or two sweaters. A pretty dress for the evening—oh, and a raincoat. Shoes and a dressing gown, undies and stockings.'

'A winter coat?'

'Oh, yes, and a coat I could wear if we went out in the evening.'

'You would like to choose the dress and coat first? Come with me, if you will…'

Two hours later Franny walked out of Harrods. Her many purchases would be sent to Wimpole Street, and all she carried was the well-known plastic bag containing a splendid selection of aids to beauty. Marc might not love her, but there was no reason why he shouldn't be proud of her. And the jars and bottles she had bought might not turn her into a beauty, but they would mitigate the plainness.

She took a taxi back to Wimpole Street and once there ate the delicious lunch Crisp had ready for her. When presently her parcels arrived, she took them up to her room and spent a delightful hour or so examining everything she had bought. She had spent a great deal of money, but not as much as the professor had allowed, and all of it, she considered, was worth every penny.

She tried on everything once more. The dress and coat were just right—very fine woollen cloth in a misty blue, and the coat had a grey imitation fur collar which exactly matched the grey of an elegant velvet hat. She had bought a jersey dress, too, in dark green, and matched it up with a top coat of green cashmere. It had been a wicked extravagance, but when she'd tried it on she'd known she had to have it... She had been more economical with the skirts and sweaters and blouses, which had then allowed her to feel justified in choosing a quilted dressing gown and a selection of flimsy undies. She had asked the sales lady to write down everything she had bought, with its price—ignoring her look of amused surprise—so that she could show it to Marc.

Later she had tea by the fire with Trimble for company, and Crisp came to tell her that the professor would be delayed but hoped to be home for dinner.

Franny was disappointed, for she was looking forward to telling Marc about her shopping. Now perhaps, if he was late home, he would be too tired to be interested. It was fortunate that Mrs Willett arrived shortly after, to tell her that he had gone back to the hospital to deal with an emergency and had told her to join Franny.

'He remembered that you were going shopping, and thought you might like to tell me about it.'

Was that a polite way of letting her know that he wasn't interested? Franny wasn't sure, but it was nice to have Mrs Willett, an enthusiastic audience of one, to admire everything.

The professor didn't return, so they dined together and then waited hopefully, but he didn't come. They wished each other goodnight and went to their beds.

Franny lay awake for a long time, listening for his return, until she slept at last, unheeding of his silent footsteps in the early hours of the morning.

He was at breakfast, immaculate in his person, placid in his good morning, although he looked tired. When Mrs Willett excused herself and they were alone, Franny produced her bill from Harrods.

'I got them to write everything down,' she pointed out, 'so that you can see just how much I spent. I bought some lovely things—'

He interrupted her impatiently. 'Quite unnecessary. Buy what you want; you have no need to bother me with the details.' He added, 'I told you how much you could spend; anything above that amount I will settle with Harrods in due course.'

He picked up a letter and began to read it, and Franny sat swallowing disappointment at his lack of interest. Presently she spoke.

'I expect you are tired and a little out of sorts if you didn't get a good night's sleep. You must try and get back earlier this evening and have an early night.'

He put down his letter. 'When I want advice as to my way of living, Franny, I shall ask for it, although I doubt that it will be you I shall consult.'

'Oh, well—I didn't mean to poke my nose into your affairs.' She added, 'It'll be difficult, I dare say, but I'll try and remember.'

He got up from the table. 'It would be as well for our future if you did.'

He nodded goodbye and went into the hall where Franny heard him talking to Mrs Willett. A minute later they left the house. She sat on at the table until Crisp came to clear away the breakfast things; she was fighting a strong feeling that she was making a mistake marrying Marc. From a logical point of view it was the sensible thing to do; he wanted a wife, she needed a home and the means to keep Auntie happy. But would it be successful? All the same, when Crisp wanted to know if he should drive her anywhere that morning she answered him cheerfully.

'I'm going out shopping again, Crisp, but I'll take a taxi to Harrods, and I think I'll have lunch out. Will you be here when I come back in the afternoon or should I take a key?'

'I shall be here, Miss Bowen; you'll be wanting tea after a long day at the shops.'

So she got ready while he fetched a taxi and was borne away once more to fill the gaps in her wardrobe. There was still enough money left from the amount Marc had told her that she might spend. She found the friendly sales lady once more and spent a long time looking at suits. She chose a smooth tweed in a mixture of autumn colours, found a cream silk blouse to wear with it, sensible but elegant low-heeled shoes and a leather handbag and gloves.

She then had the things she was wearing packed in a box with the promise of its delivery later that

day, and sailed out of the shop, feeling quite restored
in her spirits. There was money in her purse; she had
coffee and sandwiches in a small café and then went
window-shopping. She found a shirt and tie for Finn
and a bed jacket for Auntie, whom she intended to
visit on her way back to Wimpole Street. Once that
lady was up and about again, she intended to take
her shopping. New clothes, Franny decided, made
one feel a whole lot better about everything.

Her already delightful day was crowned by
Auntie's appearance when she called in at the hospital. She looked years younger, and was eager to
get back to a normal life again. Franny, on her way
back to Wimpole Street, told herself that the day had
been lovely, and resolutely ignored the memory of
Marc's impatient coolness at breakfast. He probably
has a nasty temper, she reflected, which I shall have
to learn to live with. Disregarding his instructions,
she had taken a bus back and now she was walking
down Wimpole Street.

The professor had wandered to his consulting room
windows, waiting while his nurse prepared a patient
for his examination. The street below was quiet, almost empty of traffic and people.

He saw Franny at once; she walked as though she
intended to conquer the world, and he smiled a little,
then frowned. She looked different. He studied the
fashionable suit, the elegant shoes and the handful
of smart carrier bags she was carrying, and reflected

that her new outfit had turned her into a fashionable young woman, a far cry from the Franny he had first met. He smiled again at the recollection and turned away from the window to greet his patient.

Later, driving himself to the hospital, he reflected that when he and Finn had gone to Brinsleigh he had not had the slightest intention of marrying Franny. She intrigued him, amused him, and he applauded her cheerful matter-of-fact acceptance of her life, but marrying her had been the last thing he would have thought of. Yet, when he had seen her, shabby, rather grubby and defiant, he had declared his intention of doing so. And, strangely enough, he didn't regret it.

He had been in and out of love like any other man, and at the back of his mind he had known that he would marry. But in his own time, and a carefully chosen woman who would fit into his lifestyle. He wasn't sure if Franny would fit in, but she wouldn't be at a loss as his wife. She might have lived in Fish Street but her roots were highly respectable. And there was the added bonus of the sensible relationship between them.

He would get on with his work and she would doubtless fill her days with the sort of thing wives did. They would meet in the evenings and enjoy an hour or two of each other's company, and if he had work to do she wouldn't fuss. The professor, who had had only himself to please for a number of years, was now satisfied. They liked each other and, as far as he was concerned, that was sufficient.

Later on he went back to his consulting rooms to check the next day's patients with Mrs Willett before the pair of them went upstairs to his flat.

Franny, when it became apparent that Marc wouldn't be home for tea, had changed out of the new suit and got into a dove-grey cashmere dress she had been unable to resist. It was very simple and so she had added a beautiful leather belt. It showed her pretty figure to advantage, and she had taken pains with her hair and face. Marc had told her to buy everything she needed and she had done just that. Now she would cry halt; she had enough to wear for some time.

He had been generous and she had done her best to choose clothes which would be suitable for the wife of an eminent medical man. There was still money in her purse. As soon as Auntie was out of hospital, she must have new clothes, too. Marc would pay for them—Franny had sensibly decided that he would not tolerate her aunt in shabby clothes, and he had told her that she was free to spend as much as she wanted within reason.

She would never be able to repay him, of course, but she would do her best to be the kind of wife he wanted. Not that he particularly wanted one—not one to love, at any rate. Thinking about it, she decided that on the whole they stood a good chance of making their marriage work. It wouldn't be like other marriages, perhaps, but she would do her best… And she must remember not to bother Marc with the petty details of her day. The memory of his impatience that morning still rankled.

Determined to live up to her resolve, Franny plunged at once into her new role, becoming a demure grey mouse of a girl who made no effort to start a conversation but answered her companions' remarks with pleasant composure. The professor, already taken aback at the sight of this new, elegant Franny, was at first puzzled and then amused. He had intended working in his study after dinner, but this changed Franny intrigued him, so he spent the evening in the drawing room and waited patiently for Mrs Willett to take herself off to bed.

He sat back in his chair then, watching Franny sitting rather primly in hers. She made an attempt to follow Mrs Willett but he said placidly, 'No, Franny—spare me a few minutes and tell me why you have become so unnaturally quiet. Are you upset?'

'Me, upset? No.'

'Then what has occurred to make you lose your tongue? You have had nothing to say for yourself the whole evening. May I know why?'

She folded her hands neatly in her lap and looked at him. 'Well, I'll explain. If I am to be the kind of wife you want, I must stop talking so much, mustn't I? You don't want to know about my shopping or how much I've spent, or about Crisp having a bad cold, or his sister's chilblains. Or the sales lady at Harrods who told me that her son had just been accepted at a cathedral choir school.' She looked away from him. 'You see what I mean?'

He managed not to smile. 'Yes, Franny, I do see, but I beg you not to change. I find your silence quite terrifying. I enjoy hearing you talk, and how you manage to get to know so much about people is beyond me. If you can ignore my ill-humour and just be you, you will be the kind of wife any man would wish to have. Forgive me and tell me about your shopping.'

'Really?'

'Really.'

'Well,' began Franny happily. 'I bought a suit…'

'Ah, yes, I saw it from my window when you came home this afternoon.'

'You did? Is it all right? You will tell me if you don't like any of the things I've bought?'

'I shall tell you at once and we will go together and choose something else.'

'That would be nice, but of course you would never have the time. It's nice of you not to mind me talking too much, but I don't expect you to waste your spare time. You have so little, and there must be a thousand things you want to do.'

'I can see that you will be an ideal wife,' observed the professor.

'I shall do my best,' said Franny.

'You know the kind of wife I need?' He watched her from beneath lowered lids.

'I think so. Someone who won't distract you from

your work—I mean, if you married a very beautiful woman and were madly in love with her you wouldn't have so much time for your patients, would you? So I'll do very nicely, for you don't really see me, do you? I mean,' said Franny earnestly, 'you don't look at me and think I'm the most beautiful woman in the world and how much you love me. I think I can look after your home for you and be a companion when you want one—be a background, if you see what I mean…'

He said slowly, 'Is that how you think of me, Franny? A man with a cold heart? Engrossed in his work, incapable of loving?'

'No, no. I didn't mean that at all. You just haven't been fortunate enough to meet someone to love. I dare say you will one day. You must let me know if you do; I wouldn't stand in your way. After all, our marriage is only a friendly arrangement, isn't it?'

'Franny, I think I should make myself clear—' He was interrupted by his phone. He picked it up and listened for a moment or two, then said, 'I'll come at once.'

He got to his feet. 'I must go to the hospital. We'll talk later.'

So Franny went to bed. She didn't sleep a wink because as she had watched the professor go from the room she had become aware of something. She had fallen in love with him. She had, in fact, been in love with him for some time, only she hadn't known that.

It made things very complicated, thought Franny, turning over in her bed for the tenth time. But at least it made marrying him absolutely right. It would be difficult to keep it to herself, but it wasn't as if she would see a great deal of him. And she would take care to have her own interests and not expect him to spend time with her unless he wanted to.

She hardly looked her best in the morning, but she put on the suit, did her face and hair carefully and went down to breakfast. Mrs Willett was already there, priming the professor as to his day's work.

They smiled and said good morning, and Mrs Willett bent over his diary again. 'You will just have time for a sandwich after seeing your last patient here and before you start your list at St Giles'. Then you've a consultation at four o'clock and two patients coming here at six o'clock and half past. The meeting at the Royal College of Surgeons is at eight o'clock.'

'You'll be here for dinner?' asked Franny.

'Another sandwich, Franny. I must go out again this evening—after I've attended the meeting.'

She said impulsively, 'Must you? Surely…?'

His frown stopped her. She concentrated on taking the top off her boiled egg and didn't see his look.

He had seen her shadowed eyes and faintly pink nose. 'Do you feel all right?' he wanted to know. 'You don't look quite yourself, Franny.'

'I feel marvellous,' said Franny brightly. 'Never felt better.'

He tried again, aware of a slight uneasiness. 'Have you any plans for today?'

'Oh, yes. It's so nice that it isn't raining. Rain doesn't seem to matter in the country, but it's tiresome in London, isn't it?'

She buttered toast carefully, gave him a vague smile and asked Mrs Willett if she had slept well.

She wished them both goodbye presently and went to enquire of Crisp how his cold was and wish Trimble a good day. That done, she got into her new coat and sensible shoes and took herself off for a long walk. She wouldn't be in for lunch, she had told Crisp; a day on her own getting her thoughts straight was necessary.

She ignored the buses and taxis. Instead she walked to Marble Arch, crossed the road and went into Hyde Park. At this time of the year there weren't many people about, and it was still early in the morning. It was a cold day but there was no wind and it was dry. She walked steadily, not really noticing where she went, and presently she found herself in Kensington Gardens and eventually in Kensington High Street, where she went into a café and had coffee.

There was still a lot of the day left, and she hadn't finished her thinking, but she had allowed common sense to take over from the excitement of being in love and the uncertainty of it all, and she knew now how she intended to go on.

She drank her coffee and went to the Victoria and

Albert Museum. She had been before, when she was a child, but there had never been time since then. She strolled around, allowing its vastness and displays to soothe her. She had lunch there and then started to walk back to Wimpole Street. She was tired now, but, Franny being Franny, was convinced that everything would be all right provided she kept her head.

It was strange to think that only a short time ago she and Auntie had been so unhappy at Uncle William's house. You never know what's round the corner, she thought, and allowed herself a few moments of daydreaming—Marc would discover that he was in love with her, too, and they would live happily ever after…

'Pooh!' said Franny. 'What nonsense.' She spoke in such a loud voice that a rather timid woman passing her shied away in sudden fright.

Crisp welcomed her with tea when she eventually arrived home—hot buttered toast, tiny sandwiches and a plate of fairy cakes which he modestly admitted he had baked that very afternoon.

He liked her; she had been kind and sympathetic about his cold and she had a lovely smile. He couldn't wish for a better wife for the professor. Crisp allowed his thoughts to become sentimental, under the mistaken impression that the pair of them were deeply in love.

'I understand that the professor will be out this

evening, miss. Would you and Mrs Willett like dinner at the usual time?'

'Oh, yes, please, Crisp. The professor hopes to
have a sandwich when he gets back early this evening. Could you have some ready for him? He'll
probably have missed his lunch.'

'Certainly, miss. I'll wait up until he returns this
evening. He may require something then.'

'No, don't do that. You need your sleep. I'll see
what he says when he gets here presently.' She
smiled suddenly. 'Oh, dear, I do sound bossy, don't
I? I don't mean to be.'

'Not at all, miss. If you'll let me know what he
wishes later on?'

'Of course, Crisp. The little cakes were delicious.'

Franny and Mrs Willett were sitting in the drawing
room chatting comfortably when the professor finished his consultations. It was already seven o'clock,
and although he greeted Franny cheerfully he didn't
waste time on small talk.

He looked tired. He looked tired too often, she
reflected, and asked if he would like sandwiches and
a drink.

'Yes, please—coffee, I think. Would you ask
Crisp to bring them up to my room? I'll eat while I
change.'

As he went to the door Franny asked, 'Would you
like a meal when you get home this evening? Crisp
says he'll leave something hot for you...'

'No need. The meeting should be over by nine o'clock and I've arranged to dine out.'

'Well, have a nice evening,' said Franny cheerfully. She smiled at him and wondered where and with whom he was dining, and why he didn't tell her. But why should he? She mustn't get nosy, mustn't show interest in his private life; she must remember that he wanted a wife for only one reason: to provide a suitable background and companionship.

She was having a long talk on the phone with Auntie when he came into the room again. He was in black tie and looked very splendid, she thought. She smiled and nodded at his goodnight, and when he had closed the door continued chatting with Auntie, although she had no idea of what they were talking about. All she could think of was Marc.

It won't do, she told herself, listening with half an ear to Auntie's chatter. I mustn't think about him. If he wants to tell me something, he will. Otherwise I must pretend I'm not interested.

She went down to breakfast in the morning determined to ask no questions, to hold her tongue while he read his letters and to show only polite interest in any information he might let fall concerning his day.

All wasted. Mrs Willett wasn't there—she was having breakfast in bed for a treat, Marc told her straight-faced. 'I have the licence,' he told her. 'I'm good friends with our vicar. I spent the evening with him and his wife discussing dates for our marriage. I didn't ask you to come with me because I wasn't sure if he could marry us at a moment's notice. But he is willing to do so; it is just a question of you agreeing to a suitable date and time.'

Franny opened her mouth to speak, thought better of it, and closed it again.

'I'm doing it all wrong, aren't I? But there is a problem. I arranged some time ago to go to Holland to attend my patients in various hospitals. In three days' time. Now, if you are willing, we could marry in the day after tomorrow and travel over to Holland directly afterwards. I should like you to come with me, but if you feel that I'm rushing you into something you aren't ready for say so. I'll go as arranged and we'll marry later, when I return.'

'When will that be?'

'Oh, a week or so.'

'Where would I stay while you're away?'

'Here, of course. Auntie will be here by then, too.'

'Supposing Uncle William finds out where we are…?'

The professor had nothing to say to that, and since his face wore its usual calm expression he wasn't much help.

'I think I'd like to marry you and go to Holland. What about Auntie?'

'She will be here while we are away and a very trusted nurse who works for me will come and stay here with her. And, of course, Crisp will see that she comes to no harm.'

Franny nodded. She had no doubts about that; if Marc said something would be done, then he could be believed. 'You really want me to go with you?'

He smiled again. 'Indeed, I do. Let us see—I'll bring Auntie here in time for the wedding. And we must warn Finn. He knows that he may come and go here as he wishes, but of course he must come to our wedding.'

'Where?'

'There is a small old church tucked away behind Wimpole Street. Just us? Auntie and Finn and, of course, Crisp, and I rather think that Mrs Willett will want to be there.'

Franny nodded. 'That would be very nice. Will I need a lot of clothes for Holland?'

'No, no. Take that suit and a winter coat and something pretty for the evening. You can shop as much as you want there.'

'I don't know where you live.'

'Between den Haag and Leiden. A very small village off the main roads, but most convenient for me for I work at hospitals in both cities.'

'A country house?'

'Yes. I think you will like it. Now, let us consider Auntie...'

'She'll want a new hat for the wedding.'

He managed not to smile. 'Of course. If you fetch her from St Giles' in the afternoon tomorrow? Take a taxi, of course. Go to Harrods and let her buy her hat, and, I suggest, while you are about it, a dress and coat as well. Charge it to my account.'

'I don't think that Auntie…'

'Remind her that she is about to become family, and gifts to one's family are entirely admissible.'

'You're very generous.'

He frowned. 'Nonsense. Generosity is giving away something which will deprive one. I assure you that in my case that is not so.'

'You are a very difficult person to thank,' said Franny.

'Then don't attempt to do so.' He spoke pleasantly but without interest.

A difficult man, reflected Franny, with his feelings so deeply buried that he had quite forgotten that he had any. Being married to him was going to be difficult too. If she hadn't discovered that she loved him she might have changed her mind. But she did love him…

Auntie, delighted at the idea of new clothes and a wedding, had made a splendid recovery. Assured of a secure future, and escorted by Franny, she spent an hour in Harrods where she chose a warm coat and, urged on by Franny, a fine wool dress to go under it. Choosing the hat took longer, of course, for she hadn't had a new one for a long time. But, finally satisfied, she was ushered into a taxi and driven to Wimpole Street.

Crisp was waiting for them with tea and toasted teacakes, and presently Franny took Auntie to the room she was to call her own until such time as she decided to have her own home again.

Franny settled her on her bed for a nap, then went along to her own room to inspect her own outfit with an anxious eye and then spend a long time at the dressing table, examining her face to see if the various creams and lotions she had bought had made any difference to it. Nothing noticeable, she saw with regret. But at least she had no spots and her hair gleamed with cleanliness even if it tended to be mousy.

Mrs Willett was coming to dinner and so was Finn. She got into the green jersey and, tolerably satisfied with her appearance, went along to see if Auntie was ready to go down with her.

The other three were already there when they went downstairs, and presently they sat down to the splendid dinner Crisp had cooked for them. They drank champagne, too, and there was a good deal of lively conversation. The professor was an excellent host, and Finn was in high spirits. No one mentioned the wedding, though, not until Mrs Willett took her leave to go out to the car with the professor.

'Next time we see each other it will be at your wedding.' She kissed Franny warmly. 'I wish you both every happiness.'

Franny thanked her, aware of Marc standing by her, saying nothing. Well, she thought defiantly, perhaps they would be happy; she would do her best to make it so.

When he got back Auntie went to bed and so, after a little while did Finn, who had been given a small room used as a dressing room next to Auntie's bedroom. Which left Franny and Marc alone.

Perhaps we could have a talk, she thought hopefully, get to know each other. But the professor had no such intentions. He suggested that she went to bed, too. 'I have some work I must finish this evening,' he told her, 'so I'll say goodnight.' He touched her cheek with a light finger. 'Sleep well, Franny.'

'I always sleep well,' said Franny stoutly and untruthfully. 'I hope you will, too. Goodnight, Marc.'

She took a long time getting ready for bed, quite sure that she wouldn't sleep. But the bed was warm and very comfortable, and she was tired, excited and, deep down, not very happy. Her last waking thought was that she hadn't been given an engagement ring. 'It's really too bad,' said Franny into the dark of her room, and promptly went to sleep.

But with the morning her doubts and disappointment had flown. It might not be an ideal marriage, but at least she loved Marc which was a step in the right direction.

They were to marry at eleven o'clock, have a light lunch and leave for Holland immediately afterwards. Finn and Auntie, escorted by Crisp, had already left for the church when Franny went from her room. She

and Marc were to drive to church together, and he
came out of his study as she reached the hall.

'Ready?' He smiled at her. 'You look very nice,
Franny. Cold feet?'

'Certainly not.' He looked nice, too, she thought,
in his sober grey suit and rich silk tie. She went up
to him.

'Marc, I shall do my best to be a good wife to
you, I promise you.'

He took her hand and bent and kissed her gently.
'I have no doubt about that, my dear. I believe that
we shall settle down very happily together.'

Not quite the same thing as being in love, but it
would do for the time being. She smiled up at him,
careful to keep her voice light. 'I'm sure we shall.'

She got into the car beside him and sat quietly
while he drove the short distance to the church.

It was a very small, old church, crowded out by
the buildings surrounding it, but inside it smelled of
peace and countless years of worship, and its
stained-glass windows brought colour to its grey
walls and dark pews. There were flowers too, spring
flowers arranged in the small chancel, and in the
porch Marc handed her a posy of violets, hyacinth
pips and cream rosebuds.

She walked down the aisle beside him, sure now
that everything was going to be all right; the little
church with its flowers and tranquillity told her so.

She saw Auntie and Finn, Crisp and Mrs Willett;
she saw the vicar, a fairly young man with a pleasant

rugged face; she heard his quiet voice and then Marc's and then her own; she saw the ring slipped onto her finger, and it wasn't until then that she realised that they were married.

She signed the register after Marc, kissed and was kissed, and walked back out of the church and into the car. Nothing seemed quite real, but she would doubtless remember it all later on. A dream wedding, she reflected, and tried to think of something to say to Marc.

He said easily, 'A beautiful little church, isn't it?' He sounded placid, not in the least like a just-married man.

CHAPTER EIGHT

BACK at the flat, everyone drank champagne and then sat down to an early lunch. Crisp had excelled himself, with watercress soup, poached chicken breasts with *foie gras* sauce, fresh peach sorbet and chocolate soufflé, with more champagne. The table in the elegant dining room had been decorated with a centrepiece of spring flowers and when Crisp fetched the coffee he brought in a wedding cake.

It was a delightfully informal meal, with the professor at the head of the table and Franny at its foot, Crisp on one side of her and Mrs Willett on the other, while Finn and Auntie were each side of Marc. But once they had had their coffee, Marc said, 'I don't intend to make a speech, but we would both like to thank you for coming to our wedding and giving us the pleasure of your company at lunch.'

He smiled down the table at Franny as she listened and everyone started to talk until, at a nod from him, she got to her feet. 'I hope that when we're back, we shall have another lunch together.'

She kissed her aunt and Finn, kissed Mrs Willett too, and shook Crisp's hand. 'It was a lovely meal,' she told him, 'and thank you very much, Crisp.

We're having a lovely wedding day. You'll take care of Auntie?'

'You have my word, madam. Miss Jenkins will be here shortly—that's the nurse who is to stay with us. We shall get along very well.'

They were to cross from Dover by hovercraft. Franny got into the car feeling a little muzzy from the champagne. She hoped that she wouldn't be sick on the crossing, but she thought it unlikely; she had too much to think about. Marc got in beside her, asked her if she was comfortable, then drove away, presently starting a rambling conversation which required few replies. This was a good thing, for Franny had been taken by a sudden panic.

I must have been mad, she thought wildly. I don't know anything about him and I annoy him; he's as good as said so. We should have waited, got to know each other, made quite sure... But she was quite sure, wasn't she? She loved him; she couldn't be more sure than that...

'Stop worrying, Franny.' The professor's voice was placid. 'Just enjoy yourself and leave the thinking for a few days. Take things as they come.'

Sound advice.

'I feel as though I've fallen downstairs,' said Franny.

'But you being you, Franny, I have no doubt that you will pick yourself up and be on your way, dismissing it as one of life's hazards.'

'Like getting married?'

He laughed. 'Why, yes. But I don't think that our marriage will be hazardous.' He began to tell her about Holland and den Haag.

'Your home—what is it like?'

'It's an old house. It has been added to from time to time. The village has been overlooked by road builders and estate housing simply because it lies just too far from a main road for it to be enlarged and improved.'

'It sounds nice.' It was not a very adequate answer. She waited for him to tell her more but he didn't, only asked her if she was warm enough.

He had told her very little about the journey, merely that they would be crossing to Calais and driving up through France and Belgium. The countryside looked sombre under a wintry sky, and when they reached Dover the seas looked grey and cold. But not, thank heaven, rough.

It was warm and quite comfortable inside the hovercraft, and she had a cup of tea and sat looking out at the sea, pleased to discover that she felt perfectly normal.

Do you always come this way?' she asked Marc.

'From time to time. I prefer to go from Harwich by the night ferry—it gives me more time.'

'At what time shall we get to your home?'

'This evening. We'll stop on the way for tea.'

It took a little time to thread their way out of Calais, but once on the road the Rolls made short work of getting out of France and into Belgium, and then finally into Holland. Marc stopped, then, at a cheerful little café on the side of the road, and they drank their tea—teabags in glasses of not quite boiling water, but very welcome nevertheless. They were offered a plate of *sprits* with them, a substantial buttery biscuit which Franny ate with unselfconscious pleasure. She had been too excited to eat much lunch, and dinner was still a vague meal ahead of them.

It was dark by now, and there was a faint mist drifting over the flat, open fields on either side of them. There was a good deal of traffic, too, but the professor didn't slow his pace. Not until she could see the lights of a large town ahead of them.

'Den Haag,' said Marc, and she heard the pleasure in his voice. But before they reached the town he turned off the motorway into wooded country. The road was narrow, running beside a canal and then turning away from it towards a small wood. There would be houses there, thought Franny, for she could see lights twinkling amidst the trees.

They rounded a corner and there was the village— a compact group of houses clustered round an austere church. There was no one about, only a slow-moving cart drawn by a great horse, making its way ahead of them out of the village. There were more trees here, and a high brick wall, and then an open gateway into which the professor turned. The drive ran between thick shrubberies, straight as a rule to the massive porch of the house ahead of them—a large house with a flat face and a gabled roof, its windows glowing with light.

'Not here?' asked Franny in sudden panic.

'Your—our home, Franny.' He got out and helped her from the car, and together they crossed the sweep and climbed the double steps to the front door, standing open now, with a thin, elderly man standing waiting there.

The professor clapped him gently on the back. 'Moule...' he broke into Dutch and the man smiled as he replied.

'This is Moule, Franny. He has been in the family for longer than I. He runs the place and his wife is the housekeeper. He speaks English—he was in the underground movement with my father during the occupation. Moule, this is my wife.'

Franny offered a hand and had it gently shaken.

'A delight to meet you, *mevrouw*. And here is Betke, who will take you to your room. There will be dinner in a short time.'

Betke had appeared silently at her husband's elbow to be hugged and kissed by the professor. She was almost as tall as her husband, and just as lean, but her long face with its beaky nose and bright blue eyes was friendly.

She shook hands with Franny. 'We are most happy,' she told her. 'Come with me, *mevrouw*.'

'Yes, go along with Betke,' said the professor. 'She'll show you where everything is. Come downstairs when you are ready and we'll have a drink before dinner.' He turned away as a dog, barking joyfully, came through a door and hurled itself at him.

So Franny, feeling like a guest who wasn't sure what to do next, went across the hall in Betke's wake and followed her up the wide staircase to one side. There was a half-landing where it branched to left and right to a gallery running round the hall, and Betke took the left-hand one. There were doors opening onto the gallery and several small passages. Very bewildering, thought Franny, and not at all what she had expected.

The door Betke opened revealed a large room, its long windows draped in cream brocade; the carpet was cream too. The bed was vast, a four-poster, with an old rose coverlet matching the cushions and coverings of the chaise longue and the two small easy chairs. There was a tallboy and a long table with a triple mirror upon it between the windows of some golden-coloured wood she didn't recognise. It was a beautiful room and she said so.

Betke nodded and smiled. 'And here, *mevrouw*…' She swept open a door to reveal a bathroom, far removed from the small white-tiled draughty one at Fish Street with its temperamental old geyser. This one was large and warm, and a delicate shade of pink interlarded with cream. And there was everything that a girl could possibly want. Franny gazed at the deep bath and longed to get into it. And so she would, but she was hungry, too, and besides perhaps

Marc would like her company after dinner. After all, it was their wedding day and they had hardly mentioned the fact...

Betke went away and Franny took off her hat and coat and did her face and hair. Then, feeling shy, she went downstairs.

Marc was waiting for her in the hall and she said at once, 'Oh, I hope I haven't kept you waiting?'

'No. No. Come and say hello to Biddy. She's a very placid beast although she gets rather excited when I come home.'

I shall get excited, too, thought Franny, although she didn't say so.

The drawing room rather took her breath. It was high-ceilinged and large, its walls panelled, as the dining room, but here the curtains were a rich blue brocade and the two sofas and the several armchairs were upholstered in blue and honey-coloured chintz. The hooded fireplace sheltered a log fire and there were numerous tables—lamp tables, a rent table and a sofa table behind either sofa, their mahogany gleaming with years of loving polish. Franny breathed a sigh of sheer delight.

'What a perfectly lovely room.' She turned round slowly, taking in its delights. 'Oh, and there's a cat...'

'Cato—joined us some years ago. He came in out of the rain and has been with us ever since. Come and sit down. What would you like to drink?'

'Sherry, please; dry if you have it.'

Franny went to sit on one of the sofas, but if she'd hoped that Marc would come and sit beside her she was to be disappointed. He took his drink to a wing chair on the opposite side of the fireplace and Biddy went to sit at his feet. And there was to be no intimate chat about their wedding either; instead she was given a brisk résumé of the various commitments awaiting him while they were in Holland.

He would be free tomorrow, he told her. They would go round the house and the gardens and, if she liked, walk to the village and visit the parson, or *dominee*. 'And my sisters and brother will be coming to meet you. They are all married, and I've rather lost count of my nephews and nieces. Three sisters and a younger brother, all agog to see you for themselves.'

Franny said, 'Oh,' in a worried voice. Supposing they didn't like her? Supposing she didn't like them? Although, of course, she would because they were Marc's family and she loved him... 'Your mother and father?'

'My father died of a heart attack two years ago and my mother a few months later. She had flu and then pneumonia and she really had no wish to live. They were devoted.'

'I'm sorry. Was your father a surgeon, too?'

'Yes, and his father before him. My brother is a GP in Leiden. One sister lives in den Haag; she's married to a solicitor. One is married to a vet and lives in Friesland and the youngest was married last year to the eldest son of a landowner in Limburg. We try and see each other as often as possible.'

'You're head of the family?'

'Yes. There are aunts and uncles and cousins scattered all over Holland.'

Moule came in then, to tell them that dinner was waiting, and they crossed the hall together to the dining room. The professor allowed himself a fleeting memory of the family gathering there not so long ago—Sutske had said then that perhaps the next time they met he would be a married man...

They dined off roast pheasant and red cabbage and a rich pudding with whipped cream, and they drank champagne. Franny, slightly overawed by the splendours of the dining room, nevertheless ate a good meal. She was hungry, and although people weren't supposed to have a good appetite if they were in love it didn't seem to apply to her. And for the moment, at least, she was enjoying herself; Marc could be a splendid companion if he wished.

They drank their coffee in the drawing room, on excellent terms with each other, until the professor observed that she must be tired and might like to go to bed.

She was on the point of denying this when she saw his expression. She was puzzled by it—impatience? A wish to be rid of her company? She said cheerfully, 'Oh, you won't mind? It's been rather a busy day, hasn't it? What time is breakfast?'

'Eight o'clock. Or would you rather breakfast in bed?'

'In bed?' She tried to remember when she had had such a luxury. 'No, thank you, only if I'm ill.'

She was on her feet making for the door. 'Goodnight, Marc.'

He was at the door before she reached it, holding it open. 'Goodnight, Franny. Sleep well.'

'I always sleep well,' said Franny in a voice which dared him to think otherwise. For a hopeful moment she expected him to kiss her but he didn't. She slipped past him and skimmed across the hall and up the staircase without looking back.

She got ready for bed quickly and then lay in the bath for a very long time. It was the most convenient place in which to be, for she could cry as much as she wished without having the bother of drying her eyes.

The professor went back to his chair. He had to admit that he had quite enjoyed his day. Franny had made no demands upon his attention and she had looked nice, too. Once they got to know each other he had no doubt that they would settle down nicely.

He liked her; he was even a little fond of her. He thought of her often and with pleasure. He had been in and out of love several times, but he didn't remember liking anyone as much as he liked Franny. She was inclined to say what she thought without scruple and she had a habit of talking to anyone she happened to meet in such a way that they confided in her. Like Crisp, thought the professor wryly—I didn't even notice that he had a streaming cold.

And she had faced up to bad luck and that frightful uncle of hers. It had been the least he could do to marry her and give her a secure future. The professor, who had arranged his life exactly as he wanted it for some years now, sat there arranging his future...

Franny, nicely made up, and all signs of tears ruthlessly sponged away with cold water, went down to breakfast in good spirits once more. She didn't know enough about the future to make plans; she would take each day as it came and hope for the best. The sight of Marc in casual tweeds coming in through his front door with Biddy at his heels sent her heart beating so fast that she caught her breath and stood still on the stairs. He looked up at her and smiled.

'Good morning, Franny. Did you sleep well? It's cold and dry, just right for a brisk walk later. Let's have breakfast.'

They had their meal in a small room opposite his study, a cosy room with a small fire in the steel grate, a couple of easy chairs and a small table spread with a white cloth and what she saw at once was blue delft china. Moule came in with coffee and tea, hot toast, and boiled eggs wrapped in a napkin in a pretty basket. He added another basket of various breads, marmalade in a silver dish, and at a nod from Marc went away.

Franny, while longing to be with Marc, had been nervous of meeting him again, but she need not have worried. He talked easily of the house and the village, told her a little about his family and then interrupted himself to say, 'I phoned Auntie and Finn last night. They sent their love—I told them you'd ring later. There's a phone in your room and one here, and you shall have one to carry around with you.'

She thanked him. 'I'll phone after six o'clock,' she told him. 'It's the cheap rate then—or perhaps you haven't got that in Holland?'

He assured her without the hint of a smile that, yes, there was a cheap rate in Holland too, but she was free to use the phone at any time during the day.

'Oh, silly of me. I got so used to cheese-paring I think of everything in terms of pounds and pence.'

The professor smiled then. 'Well, try and get used to thinking in *gulden* and not bothering to count them too carefully.'

They went out presently and he took her round the gardens, which were large and, even at the tail-end of winter, a joy to the eye. A terrace at the back of the house led to an expanse of lawn, lightly frosted from the cold night. Beyond that paths led to a formal Dutch garden, with a fountain at its centre and arched walks which in summer, Marc assured her, were covered in roses. And further on still, through a narrow door in the high brick wall, was the kitchen garden with a long greenhouse at its end.

He opened another door to one side and ushered her through. 'Do you ride? No? If you would like to learn there is a gentle mare here which would just suit you. Come and look at her.'

The stables were across a cobbled yard. 'This is Beauty.' Marc offered a piece of apple to the gentle-eyed horse looking at them over the stable door. He handed Franny more apple and she held it out and had it gently taken from her by velvety lips.

'Oh, she's lovely. And I'd love to learn to ride.'

'Good. This one is Thunder...'

'He's yours? He looks a bit fierce.'

'No, no. Spirited, perhaps, but a perfect gentleman.'

Thunder received his apple with a whinny and they moved on to the last door. 'Punch,' said the professor as a large equine head appeared.

'He's enormous—a shire horse... Does he work?'

'Indeed, he does. We use him at the farm; there's a home farm across the fields. He does all the work which a tractor would do. And he's as gentle as a lamb.'

They left Punch chewing on his apple, crossed the yard and went out of the barred gate leading to the open fields.

'A short cut to the village.' He glanced down at her shoes. 'It's rather muddy.'

'I'm wearing sensible shoes.' Franny beamed up at him. 'You must love your home, Marc. Don't you wish you could live here for always?'

'Frequently, but my work is important to me—the most important thing in my life—and that takes me away from home. But I have the best of both worlds, do I not? Work I love and a delightful home.'

Franny stopped suddenly. 'Do you know, I don't know how old you are?'

'Thirty-five—twelve years older than you, Franny.' 'You were a doctor—a surgeon—while I was still at school. When did you start specialising in heart surgery?'

'Eight years ago.'

'And you never wanted to marry?'

'I never felt the need, not for some years.'

'Is that why you married me? Because I was in a jam and needed help?'

He stood beside her, looking down at her upturned face.

'Yes, but having said that I must tell you that it is something I shall never regret, Franny.'

'You might fall in love...'

'If I can find the time and inclination. The possibility is so remote that I believe it is something we need not concern ourselves with.'

He tucked her hand under his arm. 'How serious we have become. Let us go to the village and call upon the *dominee*.'

He was a delightful man, Franny discovered, with a wife not much older than herself and twin boys, toddlers, as well as a very young baby girl. They had coffee together and talked about the wedding, the village and its inhabitants, some of the time excusing themselves and speaking their own language. The parson spoke excellent English and his wife had more than a smattering—enough to have a pleasant chat with Franny. 'You must learn Dutch,' she told her.

This was something Franny hadn't thought about until that moment. Of course she would have to learn, even if Marc didn't live in Holland all the time. When he retired he—they—would live here permanently. And by then, she reflected, he might love her.

They walked through the village on the way home and it seemed to her that Marc knew every single person living in it. She shook hands and smiled, and when someone spoke English replied thankfully. But mostly she was addressed in Dutch, which meant that she could only murmur suitably.

They spent the afternoon wandering round the house, stopping very often to examine the family portraits on its walls. The men of the family all looked alike and their ladies, she was glad to see, were on the whole small and undistinguished, although they looked happy. The portraits of his father and mother hung in the hall—his father an older edition of Marc, his mother with a sweet face and cosily plump.

'I'm sorry I didn't know them,' said Franny as she followed the professor up the staircase.

There were a great many rooms, large and small,

some facing onto the gallery, some lurking down narrow passages, but all of them charming and splendidly furnished.

'There must be an awful lot of housework,' said Franny. 'Does Betke have plenty of help?'

'Oh, yes. I don't know exactly how much; there are maids who live here and I believe someone comes up from the village each day. You must talk to Moule about that.'

He sounded indifferent and she felt snubbed. Was she expected to act as mistress of his home, she wondered, or as an occasional visitor?

That evening he told her that on the following day he would be going to den Haag and that if she wished she might like to go, too.

'I shall be at the hospital all day, but I'm sure you will find plenty to do. There are some good shops and I expect you can find something you like. We will have to leave quite early—just after eight o'clock.'

'I should like that very much. I won't be a nuisance?'

'No, no, of course not. I'll drop you off close to the shopping streets. I shall be at the main hospital. I'll write the name and address down for you; all you need to do is take a taxi there. I should be finished by five o'clock. If I'm not, go to the reception and tell them who you are—someone will let me know you're waiting.'

*   *   *

Franny wore the green coat and dress to go to den Haag, and the small felt hat she had bought to match them. Shopping would be fun, and she was sure that there would be plenty to see—museums and picture galleries. She got into the car beside Marc, ready to enjoy her day. She had her instructions safe in her bag and she was to buy anything she wanted.

It wasn't until she was standing on the pavement by the Ridderszaal, watching the Rolls disappear into the traffic, that she realised that she had no money. She opened her handbag and searched through it. A handful of English coins, a ten-pound note and nothing else. She toyed briefly with the idea of going to the hospital and asking Marc for some money and then dismissed it; he would be in Theatre or on a ward round, taking a clinic or seeing patients. He would be nice about it but it would annoy him. His work, she reminded herself, was all-important. Well, she had ten pounds; she would change it and keep it for lunch and a taxi.

It was still early and the shops were barely open. She wandered round looking in their windows. They were elegant shops and she saw several things she would have liked to buy. She told herself that at least she would know where to come another time, and decided to have coffee. It was a small, pleasant café, and she drank her coffee slowly, ate the little biscuit with it and planned what she could see would be a long day.

The VVV—the tourist office—was just across the

street. A map would be a good idea, and some information as to the museums and interesting buildings. If she spent the morning looking at the shops, and had a sandwich lunch, she could spend the afternoon at one or other of the museums and then get a taxi.

The waitress offered her the bill and stood smiling. Surely there was a mistake? thought Franny. Such a small cup of coffee to cost more than two pounds? She paid from the small stock of *gulden* she had got from the bank and added a tip. Lunch would have to be a meagre affair.

There were several large stores close by, so she spent a long time in each of them, for it was warm inside and there was plenty to look at. The VVV had given her a map and recommended the Mauritshuis museum, and had told her that the entrance fee was very small. By midday she was hungry and her feet ached, but she had learned her lesson.

She walked around until she found a café crowded with people drinking coffee and eating *broodjies*. She found a place at a table and sat a long time over her cheese roll and coffee. She would have liked another cup of coffee, but she would need her last few *gulden* to take her to the hospital.

At the museum she queued for a ticket, and as it turned out the 'small' fee took most of her remaining money. There was nothing she could do about that. There were trams; one of them must go to the hospital or at least near it. She told herself not to worry and spent the next few hours enjoying the marvellous paintings the museum housed. On the way out she stopped to ask the attendant at the door where she should go for a tram to the hospital and, armed with directions, made her way back to the main streets.

The evening rush hour was just starting and she had to queue for a tram. The queue disintegrated when the tram arrived and it was everyone for himself. Franny, swept on board by powerfully built men and sturdy housewives, got her purse out.

But there wasn't enough money in it. The conductor frowned and shook his head at her and, since she couldn't understand a word he was saying, she waved the paper Marc had given her in his face. It was an elderly man sitting nearby who came to her aid. He spoke to the conductor, who took what money she had and gave her a ticket. The elderly man said, 'You have a ticket to take you some of the way. Get off when he tells you; it is not far to walk.'

Franny thanked him and in a little while, obedient to the conductor's nod, got off the tram. It was a main street, she was relieved to see, and the conductor pointed ahead of her and waved an arm. All she needed to do was walk until she saw the hospital. This was a different part of den Haag entirely, with dark buildings on either side of the street and a great many people going home from work. It became darker and busier as she walked. Factories, she supposed, or offices, which were empty now, their lights extinguished. She stopped a woman coming towards her, and held out her paper. 'The hospital?'

The woman glanced at the paper. She waved an arm behind her and hurried on so Franny set off again. It couldn't be all that far away—at least the girl had known the place. But it took another fifteen minutes before she saw the hospital looming ahead of her.

She crossed the forecourt, went through the entrance into the vast reception hall and saw Marc at once. He came to meet her, his face impassive although he glanced at his watch. He said, 'I was starting to worry—what held you up?'

Franny wished very much to fling herself on his massive chest and have a good cry, but instead she said in a matter-of-fact voice, 'Lack of money.'

'Lack of…' The look of consternation on his face made her feel better. 'My dear girl—good God! I left you to spend the day without a *gulden*. How you must hate me… Had you no money at all?'

'I had ten pounds, which I changed into *gulden*, and I don't hate you. I quite often forget things myself; it's quite a normal thing to happen to anyone. And you had a good deal to think about, I dare say.'

'Franny, don't heap coals of fire on my head. I am sorry.' He caught her arm. 'Come with me. You shall have a cup of tea and tell me how you managed.'

He led her away from the reception desks and

down a passage to a small room, where he picked up a house phone from the table. A tray of tea came within minutes. The professor sat her down in one of the vast leather chairs and handed her a cup.

'I'll see my bank manager tomorrow and get you a chequebook.' He took her handbag from the table and stuffed a bundle of notes inside. 'And that must do to go on with. Forgive me, Franny?'

'Of course I forgive you…'

'Then tell me how you managed all day with—what was it?—ten pounds—good Lord, that's barely enough for a cup of coffee in this town.'

'Yes, it's expensive, isn't it? But the shops are lovely.'

She told him how she had spent her day, and when she had finished he said, 'I promise you this will never happen again, Franny. Tell me, did you not think of telephoning here and asking for me?'

'Yes, of course I did. But for all I knew you were in Theatre or doing a ward round,' she said earnestly. 'If it had been really important, like breaking a leg, then I would have let you know.'

He looked at her unassuming features, which were quite cheerful now. He had always known that she was someone who would face up to difficulties; she had common sense and a matter-of-fact approach to any obstacle, and she didn't burst into tears when something went wrong. He was, he admitted to himself, getting quite fond of her.

He went to hospital again the following morning,

but returned for lunch and then drove Franny to den Haag to meet his eldest sister. She lived with her husband and three small children in an old, gabled house in a quiet street close to the town's heart. She was a tall girl with her brother's blue eyes and high-bridged nose. She welcomed them warmly while the children milled around with Biddy and his sister's two dogs. It was a roomy house, beautifully furnished, and Elsa, his sister, took Franny on a tour of it.

'We are all so delighted Marc has married,' she told Franny. 'He's such a splendid man—but you know that already—and he loves children.' She didn't see Franny's pink cheeks. 'We're all coming to dinner on Saturday. It's funny, Sutske—that's my youngest sister—said at Christmas that she hoped that the next time we were all together Marc would have a wife. And here you are!' She beamed at Franny. 'Mother and Father would have loved you.'

The professor informed them that he had one more day at the hospital. 'Oh, good,' said Elsa. 'Bring Franny here. We'll go shopping and you can come back here when you've finished at the hospital.'

A happy suggestion which became a happy day. Franny, with money in her purse now and a cheque-book besides, was taken from one boutique to another and returned presently with two new dresses, a pair of shoes she hadn't been able to resist, and a rather beautiful leather handbag.

They had tea at Elsa's house before returning home and, although Marc went to his study to work again after dinner that evening, Franny was happy; they were getting to know each other.

When Saturday came she dressed in one of the new dresses—a dark red velvet, elegantly cut and simple—for the dinner party, and when she went down to the drawing room Marc was there, waiting for her.

'My mother's ring,' he told her, slipping a great sapphire and diamond ring onto her finger above her wedding ring. 'And this…' He opened a case and took out a pearl necklace. 'A belated wedding gift.'

He fastened it around her neck and dropped a kiss onto her cheek. 'I am a shockingly bad husband; you should have had these when we married.'

It was hard to find the right answer to that; Franny thanked him prettily and felt relief when their guests arrived.

She felt a little overwhelmed at first—there were so many of them and since they all wished to talk to her at once she had difficulty in sorting them out. It didn't matter, though; the warmth of their welcome into the family was sincere and presently she began to enjoy herself.

Sitting opposite Marc at the splendidly decked dinner table, she felt the first gleam of hope that they were going to be happy, she and Marc. Perhaps not the wildly romantic happiness of those in love, but a secure and lasting affection on his part and her love for him—which he need never know of.

The last guest went just after midnight, and they went back to the drawing room to sit for a while.

'When we come next time—some time in the late spring—we will visit the family. It is a pity that I am tied up for the next few days.'

'At the hospital here?'

'No, Utrecht and then Rotterdam. I won't ask you to come with me; you would be alone for most of the days. Would you be happy to stay here?'

She assured him that she would, for that was the answer he expected. And as it turned out she wasn't in the least bored; she took Biddy for long walks and went to the village, making friends with the people there even though she did not understand a word anyone said. She lunched with the *dominee* and his wife and invited them to tea. The days passed happily enough and Marc telephoned each evening, the high spot of her day.

When he got back she greeted him with reserved pleasure, afraid to show her feelings. They were to return to London in two days' time, he told her.

'Shall we have a look around the country? And we might dine out and dance. There are some good hotels in den Haag.'

They spent a happy hour or two deciding how they would spend their last days, and as Franny got up to go to bed the professor said, 'I have been looking forward to coming home and finding you waiting for me, Franny.'

He kissed her on the top of her head as she went past him, and she stopped and looked up at him. 'That's the nicest thing anyone has ever said to me.'

She went down to breakfast after a dreamless night. Life was quite perfect—well, almost perfect. It would get better, she assured herself.

Actually it got worse, and all at once. Marc wasn't in the breakfast room and Biddy was sitting disconsolate by his empty chair. There was a note by her plate. He had been called away in the very early hours of the morning on an emergency—the VIP in Brussels. He was flying there at once; he would phone as soon as possible.

He rang that evening. He had operated on his patient, who was expected to recover; he would stay in Brussels for another day and then drive back late in the evening. He would pick her up and they would board the Harwich Ferry. And would she ask Moule to come to the phone?

So it was more long walks with Biddy, and more long hours filled with wandering round the house, getting to know it. She was disappointed, but she was sensible enough to know that a medical man's wife had to fit in with his work without fussing.

When he got home on the last evening she was quite ready to leave. They had a light supper, took Biddy for a last brisk walk while he told her about his patient, and then drove to the Hoek and boarded the ferry.

The professor hadn't apologised for leaving her alone but she hadn't expected him to; it was his work and he had made it clear that his job was the most important thing in his life. She drew comfort from the fact that he was pleased to see her. He wasn't a demonstrative man, but she had welcomed the weight of his arm when he flung it round her shoulder.

CHAPTER NINE

IT WAS raining as Marc began the drive up to London from Harwich. It had been a fairly smooth crossing and he and Franny had had breakfast on board before they disembarked. They should be home by mid-morning, observed Marc. 'I must go to St Giles' directly after lunch, and I have several patients to see at my consulting rooms in the evening. You will be glad to see Auntie again. I wonder if Finn will be able to get away for a while?'

'I phoned him while you were in Brussels. He's hard at work, he says, but he'll ring one evening. I hope he's not working too hard...'

'I imagine he manages the odd hour or two in which to enjoy himself,' said the professor dryly. 'I did.'

Crisp was waiting for them, his round face beaming.

'There's coffee ready to pour,' he assured them, 'and Mrs Blake in the drawing room. I'll fetch the bags. Will you be needing the car, sir?'

'After lunch. No need to take it round to the garage. Everything all right, Crisp?'

'No problems, sir. The letters are in your study, and I've noted down the phone calls.'

'Splendid. Let's go and see Auntie…'

He had taken off his coat and now he took Franny's, cast them over a chair, took her arm, opened the drawing room door and crossed to where Auntie was sitting.

Auntie got up quite briskly. 'My dears, how lovely to see you again. Did you have a good time in Holland? I'm longing to hear all about it. Crisp has been so good to me, and that nice woman, Miss Jenkins—what a pleasant person she is. She's coming to see you later, I was to tell you.'

While she talked she hugged Franny and lifted her face to the professor for his kiss. 'I've done my exercises,' she told him, 'and walked every day. And Finn has been to see me…'

She was interrupted then, by Crisp with the coffee tray, and presently Marc excused himself with the plea that he had to read his post. So Franny, with Auntie to keep her company, unpacked and told her about Holland and Marc's lovely home and the people she had met.

'You're happy, love?' asked Auntie.

'Yes, Auntie, I am. Marc is a very kind and considerate man.' She gave a small sigh. 'He works too hard, though.'

'Only because he has had no reason to do otherwise,' said Auntie sensibly. 'Now he's a married man he will have you to think of and, later on, children! He'll still work hard, but it won't be the be-all and end-all of his life.'

If only that could be so, reflected Franny, but moaning about it wasn't going to help. She agreed cheerfully and added, 'Marc says I am to take you to Harrods and you are to buy what you would like to wear. Shall we go tomorrow? He's going to be busy all day.'

'Harrods? But that's such an expensive shop, dear.'

'He said Harrods,' observed Franny, 'so I think we'd better go there.'

It seemed to her, now that they were back at Wimpole Street, that Marc had become remote. He was pleasant and friendly, but from a distance, as it were. She had thought once or twice in Holland that they were closer together, that there was a chance that they would become something more than friends, but now she wasn't so sure. Anxious not to betray her own feelings, she became a little cool towards him while doing her best to be the kind of wife he wanted.

It wasn't easy, and once or twice Auntie looked at her in a puzzled fashion, although she said nothing. They had had their shopping expedition, and, at first with reluctance and then with growing pleasure, Auntie had chosen the kind of clothes she had never expected to wear again. Going back in the taxi, she had observed that Marc was just about the nicest man she had ever met—'Except for my husband,' she had added. 'And so devoted to you, love.'

If only he were, Franny had thought, but had said brightly that he was indeed devoted. And if that meant giving her a handsome allowance, taking an interest in her day when he got home in the evening and telling her from time to time in a rather absent-minded manner that she looked nice, then, yes, he was devoted.

They had been back for a week when he told her that they were to dine with Lady Trumper.

'No,' said Franny without even stopping to think. 'I won't go.'

He raised his eyebrows. 'You are my wife, Francesca. I am not ashamed of you—why should you be?'

'I'm not in the least ashamed,' she said fierily. 'But I do not like Lady Trumper and she doesn't like me.'

'I'm afraid that you will have to meet and even entertain a good many people you don't like, my dear. It is for Thursday, seven-thirty for eight-o'clock. Wear something pretty; you can look very nice, you know.'

He had smiled gently and went away, leaving her to rage around the flat so that Auntie and Crisp exchanged several worried glances.

'What has upset you, Franny?' asked Auntie over the tea tray Crisp had brought a little earlier than usual, in the hope that a nice cuppa would clear the air.

Franny told her aunt, but if she had expected a sympathetic reply she didn't get one.

'My dear child, what could be better? A chance for you to let Lady Trumper see that you are as good as she is, if not a great deal better. After all, our family is an old one—William the Conqueror, my dear—a good deal better than hers.' Auntie snorted delicately. 'After all, what was her husband? Knighted for making nuts and bolts for tanks or something? New money, my dear. She's a snob. Tomorrow we will go to Harrods and you shall buy a really lovely dress.'

'You think it will be all right if I go? I don't want to shame Marc.'

'I think that would be impossible.'

So back they went to Harrods, to the sales lady who was beginning to consider herself a friend by now. A suitable dress for a dinner party? Something dignified? She had just the thing.

It looked a mere handful of glistening amber chiffon hanging over her arm, but on Franny's shapely person it was transformed into a thing of beauty. And it was a perfect fit. Its price shocked Franny, but she reminded herself that Marc had told her to get something pretty... This was more than pretty, it was exquisite, and it really transformed her from a rather plain girl into a young woman who would surely attract a second or even a third glance. Franny bore it home and said nothing to Marc.

*   *   *

He was late home on the evening of the dinner party. Franny, sitting in the drawing room, the few lamps she had switched on giving just sufficient light to show up the beauty of the dress, was disappointed when he thrust his head round the door with a quiet, 'Hello. Ready, are you? Good. I'll not be long.'

She was in the hall already wrapped in her long velvet coat when he returned. His brisk, 'Good girl. Quite ready?' was curt, and at her nod he ushered her down the stairs to the front door and opened the car door for her.

There wasn't a great deal of traffic and it was no great distance. Barker opened the door to them on their arrival and Franny wished him good evening in a pleasant voice and allowed him to take her coat. The professor, shrugging his own coat off, gave her a brief, reassuring glance and then stood stock-still as the glance became a long look.

How was it that he had never noticed how pretty she was? And the dress showed off her person to its fullest advantage. He had a sudden wish to take her in his arms and tell her so, but with Barker standing there it wasn't possible. But the smile he gave her spoke more than words; Franny, her small chin in the air, her feet on cloud nine, accompanied him into the well-remembered drawing room.

There were a number of persons there; they parted to allow their hostess, majestic in slightly too tight black satin, to cross the room to greet Marc and Franny.

The professor pecked her cheek. 'Of course, you know my wife, Francesca,' he said easily, and Franny shook hands and smiled and murmured prettily for all the world as though she had never set eyes on Lady Trumper before. There was a great deal she would have liked to say, but she must remember that she was Marc's wife…

Marc knew most of the other guests; they congratulated him on his marriage and spoke kindly to Franny, liking her quiet manner and pleasant voice. She sipped Lady Trumper's indifferent champagne and answered their friendly questions with a readiness which charmed them. Lady Trumper, talking to the professor, eyed her across the room.

'Who would have thought it?' she began.

'Who, indeed?' His voice was cool as he went on to ask her how she had been since he had seen her.

'You can't love her—she's managed to catch you…'

'Shall we consider that remark unsaid?' He spoke quietly, his voice icy now. He turned and walked away and joined the group around Franny, and then, unnoticed, left the room. There was a phone in the hall; his call was brief.

Barker was on the point of announcing dinner when the phone rang and he went to answer it. Instead of giving the expected summons to the table he crossed the room to the professor and murmured in his ear.

Marc said, 'I'm wanted on the phone; so sorry to delay things. Why not go in without me?'

They were indeed going unhurriedly to the dining room when he touched Franny on the shoulder. 'I'm sorry, Franny, I'm wanted, I'm afraid. I must go at once.' He smiled at the looks and murmurs of sympathy. 'Would you like to stay?'

She gave him such a speaking look that he almost laughed out loud. 'If Lady Trumper wouldn't mind, I'd like to come with you. It might be something…'

She was saved from inventing the something by his brisk reply. 'Then let us bid Lady Trumper goodbye at once.'

She looked up at him. 'It's very urgent?'

'Yes.'

Amid a chorus of regretful goodbyes they made their apologies and said their farewells to Lady Trumper, and if Franny thought that Marc was curt in his manner she put it down to his anxiety to get to the hospital. Barker, looking almost human, wrapped her coat around her and bowed them out, and Franny was bustled into the car.

She kept quiet for a few minutes while Marc drove and then she ventured, 'Are you going straight to the hospital? I can easily get a taxi from there.'

'We're going home…'

'Auntie—oh, why didn't I guess? It's Auntie! Can't you drive faster, Marc?'

'Auntie, to the best of my knowledge, is in good health. We will stop for a few minutes while I speak to Crisp and then we will spend the evening dining and dancing.'

Franny turned to look at him. 'Marc, I don't understand. Isn't there a patient?'

'No.'

'But why have we left?'

He spoke in the same quiet, cold voice which had shaken Lady Trumper. 'I do not choose to stay under the roof of anyone who insults me.'

'Not Lady Trumper? Insulting you? I can't imagine anyone doing that...' She frowned. 'Did she insult you or was it me?'

He turned his head to look at her. 'Anyone who insults you, insults me, Francesca.'

'Oh, dear, I'm sorry. It's spoilt your evening. And what a waste of a new dress. I very nearly didn't buy it, it was so expensive. I wish I hadn't now.'

'I'm very glad you did buy it. It is a beautiful dress and you look lovely in it. We'll go and show it off on the dance floor.'

'Well, I never,' said Franny chattily. 'And, do you know, I thought you never noticed what I was wearing?'

She was silent then, digesting the fact that he had said that she looked lovely. He hadn't meant it, of course, but it was nice all the same...

At the flat they went in together, and Franny told Auntie in a few breathless sentences what had happened while the professor went in search of Crisp.

He was only gone for a few minutes; she bade

Auntie a happy goodbye and got back into the car with Marc. She wondered if there would be a table for them without a previous booking, but she didn't ask.

They were given a splendid table at the restaurant Marc chose and, conscious that she looked her best, Franny accepted a glass of champagne and then studied the menu. With quiet prompting from the professor she chose darioles of salmon à la Muscovite, roast wild duck with orange sauce and then a Milanaise soufflé.

She ate the salmon with unselfconscious pleasure, and the professor, watching her with an equal pleasure, suggested that they might dance before the duck was served.

'I haven't danced for years,' said Franny, but she got up promptly and slid into his arms, as light as thistledown. In earlier, happier years, she had danced a lot. It was like riding a bicycle—once learned, never forgotten.

As for the professor, he became aware that, now that Franny was in his arms, he had no wish to let her go…

They ate the duck, drank the champagne and danced again before the soufflé. After their meal the professor lifted a finger and the waiter was at their table in a twinkling. Marc was a man who would always receive attention at once, thought Franny, watching him tell the man that they would have coffee later.

By mutual consent they danced again, and went on dancing, and after they had drunk their coffee Marc said, 'One more dance before we go home?'

'Do you have to go to the hospital tomorrow?' asked Franny, craning her neck to see his face.

'Yes, I've a list starting at nine o'clock, a clinic in the afternoon and a patient to visit on my way home.' He didn't say more than that.

They talked about their evening casually as they drove home, and it wasn't until they were in the drawing room that Franny said, 'I'm sorry about this evening—I mean, Lady Trumper. It was very unpleasant for you.'

'I had quite forgotten about her,' he told her placidly, which wasn't true, of course. He would have liked to wring the woman's neck...

'Oh, good. Thank you for a lovely evening.'

'It is I who must thank you, Franny. We must do it again sometime.'

She wished him goodnight then, and went up to her room because she could see that he didn't want her there any longer. Not that he had given any sign of it; she supposed it was because she loved him that she was instinctively aware of that.

She stood for a long time in front of the pier glass in her bedroom, studying her reflection. The dress was perfect—it had been worth every penny. And later, ready for bed in her nightie, her hair hanging loose around her shoulders, she went and had another look at the dress hanging in the closet. It might be a long time before she wore it again.

As it turned out that seemed likely. Marc, home late after a long day, told her that he would be leaving in a few days' time to go on a lecture tour. 'I go in three or four days,' he told her, 'after I deal with appointments already made and take an afternoon clinic.'

She made her voice merely friendly. 'Will you be away long?'

'A week or ten days; I'll be in Israel.'

She forgot to be merely friendly. 'Marc—but it's not safe there—supposing…? Oh, do be careful. Must you go?'

'Yes, it is a long-standing commitment.' He was staring at her. 'I shall be quite safe, Franny.'

She ventured, 'You wouldn't like me to come with you?'

'Very much, but, no, I think not.'

She reminded herself that it was his work; that was what mattered to him, never mind the hazards which went with it. She said in a bright voice, 'I dare say you'll be able to phone…'

'Oh, yes. Will you miss me, Franny?'

She bent her head over an imaginary piece of fluff on her skirt. 'Oh, yes, of course I shall. We shall all miss you.'

She was quite unable to still the little quiver in her voice as she spoke.

'While I am away there is something I should like you to do. I have bought the mews cottage next door to the garage behind the house. I believe that Auntie might like to live there, don't you? It would be another home for Finn, if he should feel like it. Would you take her over there and see what she thinks?'

'Marc—she'll love it. She'll have her own home again.' She added doubtfully, 'She's very independent.'

'I realise that. Try and make her see that I regard her as family and remind her that families share amongst themselves.'

'Very well, I'll do my best. Do you want to tell her about it?'

'Not before I leave. I'm going to be early away and late home for the next few days.'

He was shutting her out, politely and kindly. Most wives would have been fussing around, packing his bag, reminding him to look after his passport and to let her know the minute he arrived and above all to take care. But she wasn't that kind of wife. Crisp would pack his bag and there was a note on the pad on his desk—exactly where he would be, phone numbers if he should be wanted urgently, a number she could ring if necessary.

He was to leave for Israel very early that morning. Franny, pattering along to the dining room in her dressing gown, found him at the table, with Crisp offering toast and more coffee. She sat down and took the coffee he offered her and wished them both good morning, adding that it looked as though it was going to be a fine day.

It was an optimistic remark, since the sun was barely above the horizon, but it was something to say. She wished very much she could tell him to come home quickly and safely because she loved him and to be without him was intolerable, but of course that would never do. She voiced the thought out loud.

'What a pity one may not say exactly what one wants to say. I mean, who cares about the weather? All the thoughts inside one's head which may not be uttered...' The professor put down his cup, aware at last that all his efforts not to fall in love with Franny had been in vain. He said softly, 'Francesca...'

Too late. Crisp came back into the room to say that the car was outside and the professor was cutting it fine if he wanted to get his flight.

The professor looked at Franny, rosy from sleep, her hair all over the place, and knew suddenly that there was a great deal more to life than work. There was love—and unfortunately no time to tell her so. He got up, bent and kissed her hard and went away.

Franny sat and thought about that kiss; she hadn't been kissed very often and never like that. He would be back in ten days' time at the latest; perhaps he would kiss her again. She mustn't get too excited, she told herself, he might have been carried away on the spur of the moment.

She told Auntie about the mews cottage later that day, and, once she had got over her surprise and expressed herself unable to live on Marc's bounty, Auntie consented to go and see it.

'But I refuse to be beholden to the dear man, Franny. He has done so much for us already and he's so good with Finn—like a big brother.'

'You'll stay with us, then?' asked Franny cunningly.

'Good gracious, no. I am here as a guest, but only for the moment.'

'But when it was suggested that you might like to live somewhere near us you were quite pleased.'

'I wasn't quite myself. After all, I have my pension; I can find a bed-sitting room.'

They fell silent, because of course that was nonsense. Presently Franny said, 'Auntie, Marc is going to be deeply hurt if you refuse his offer. He thinks of you as family—and he saved your life, didn't he? Now he wants to see you enjoying it again. Don't you see that if you go off somewhere on your own he will be worrying about you? He works so hard and worries enough about his patients, although he never says so. He shouldn't have to worry about us as well. We're his family now, to make his home really home, and not just a place where he comes back to sleep and eat.'

Auntie sat up very straight. 'I have been selfish

and foolish. It would be delightful to live in my own little house and yet be close to you.'

Franny got up and gave her a hug. 'Good. Let's go now; it's only a couple of minutes' walk.'

The cottage was delightful. Crisp had given Franny the keys and she opened its small door into a tiny hall and then a living room. There was a small kitchen and a little staircase leading to two bedrooms and a bathroom. It was in good repair—the walls distempered, the floors sound.

'Marc said you were to choose the decorating and the furniture. Crisp will arrange for someone to come with wallpaper and samples; you only have to tell him.'

'You mean, I can start straight away?'

Franny nodded. 'Just tell Crisp what you want; it seems he can arrange for the decorators to start as soon as you wish.'

'I can't believe it,' said Auntie. And then, 'A pretty wallpaper in the living room, and pale yellow walls in the kitchen. Carpets?'

'Fitted everywhere, don't you think? And curtains…?'

Auntie was weeping happily. 'My dear, I never thought to be as happy as this again. Fish Street and then William and being ill—they're like a bad dream.'

'You'll have made Marc happy too,' said Franny.

Despite the hustle and bustle of organising the cottage the days dragged for Franny. The professor had phoned from Israel; he had had a good flight, he told her, the hotel was comfortable, he would be there for three days and then he was going on his tour. And he had rung again some days later. The tour was successful so far; he hoped to be back in five days' time.

Franny crossed the days off the kitchen calendar like a child.

The last day came, and she phoned the airport to check the time of arrival. The flight had been delayed, she was told. A lightning strike had upset the schedule and, no, at the moment they had no idea at what time the plane would arrive. At midnight, still without news, Franny went to bed with Crisp's promise that he would wake her the minute the professor returned. She stayed awake for some time, before she finally fell into a heavy sleep and woke to find broad daylight. She flung on her dressing gown and met Crisp in the hall.

'He's back?'

'Yes, madam, four o'clock this morning. There is a note for you on the breakfast table.'

'You promised to wake me, Crisp.'

'The professor forbade me, madam. He said on no account were you to be disturbed until you woke.'

'But where is he?'

'At the hospital. Left here at six o'clock. He was asked for urgently.'

'But he hasn't been to bed. He'll be exhausted…'

'If I may say so, madam, the professor is never exhausted. He tells me he slept on the flight, and I gave him a good breakfast.'

'Crisp, you're a treasure, and thank you. Did he say when he was coming home?'

'It depends on what he finds at the hospital.'

'I'd like to ring him but I won't; he'll be busy. I'll get dressed, anyway. You must be tired, Crisp. I could cook my own breakfast. Why don't you go and rest for a bit?'

'I had sufficient sleep, madam. Thank you for the kind thought. I will take a brief nap this afternoon. A nice dish of scrambled eggs for you and Mrs Blake? In twenty minutes or so?'

Franny took Marc's note back to her room and sat down to read it on the bed. It was short and businesslike: he had been called to St Giles' urgently and might be delayed for some time. That was all. She read it through several times, trying to breathe warmth into the few words without success. He would come home just as soon as he could, she told herself.

She spent the morning helping Auntie to choose material for curtains and had a long talk with Finn on the phone. Life was great, he assured her, and he'd met this girl—a fellow student.

'I told Marc about her and he said to bring her along to meet us one evening. You'll like her.'

'I'm sure I shall,' said Franny warmly. 'Have you known each other long?'

'Last week.'

'So how did Marc know about her?'

'Well, I told him, didn't I? Saw him this morning at St Giles'; he'd been in Theatre.'

'Yes, of course,' said Franny. 'He had to go in early. He had hardly any sleep—didn't get home till the early hours.'

'He looked on top of the world.'

Franny thought about that later. What reason would he have for that? The tour had been successful, but he wasn't a man to broadcast his success, and if it had been something really marvellous why hadn't he woken her up and told her?

She pecked at her lunch, saw Auntie into bed for her afternoon nap and went to look out of the window. The Rolls was in the street below. Marc was back, seeing patients in his rooms. He would be coming as soon as he had finished there.

She went along to the kitchen, and, since Crisp had gone to his room to catch up on his sleep, she cut sandwiches—Gentleman's Relish, cucumber, and egg and cress—and arranged some of Crisp's little cakes on a dish.

That done, and unable to sit still, she went back to the window. The Rolls was still there. She went off to her room and did her face again and tidied her already neat hair, and then took another peek from the window.

'This is silly,' she told herself, and went and sat down as far away from the window as possible, leafing through a magazine until Crisp came to ask her at what time she would like tea.

'Well, I see the professor's in his rooms; I thought we'd wait for a while in case he comes.' She added apologetically, 'Crisp, I made some sandwiches, I hope you don't mind.'

He gave her a fatherly smile. 'A splendid idea, madam, the professor enjoys a sandwich. No doubt very welcome after all that eastern food he's had to eat.'

Auntie came in presently, picked up her knitting and began to talk about the cottage. Once or twice she glanced at the handsome carriage clock on its wall bracket; it was past tea time and she longed for a cup of tea. She asked presently, 'Has Marc been home, dear?'

'Not here. He's been in his rooms all the afternoon, though. I expect he'll come soon. I thought we'd wait tea…'

But when five o'clock struck and there was no sign of Marc, they had their tea and Auntie, at least, enjoyed the sandwiches. Franny drank her tea and got up to look out of the window once more. Mrs Willett was leaving the house. That meant there were no more patients. She heaved a sigh of relief and sat down again, her ear straining to hear his key in the door.

But he didn't come, and after another half-hour she went to the window yet again. The Rolls was there, so he was alone in his rooms. She was sure of

that for he never saw patients unless his nurse or Mrs
Willett were there. And his nurse had been given a
holiday while he was away.

She said suddenly, 'I'm going down to the rooms.
It's time Marc had his tea.'

On the landing below, the waiting-room door was
closed but not locked. She crossed the empty room,
hesitated for a moment and then opened his consulting room door.

The professor was sitting at his desk. It was piled
with papers—patients' notes, reports on tests, pam-
phlets and letters—but he was occupied with none
of them; he was occupied with his thoughts. He
looked up as Franny went in and got to his feet.

'Franny, is something wrong?'

She walked up to the desk, took one of the chairs
set ready for patients and folded her hands tidily in
her lap.

'Yes,' she said. 'You came home early this morning, you wouldn't let Crisp call me—and he had
promised, you know—you had to go to St Giles',
but you've been here since just after twelve o'clock.
Mrs Willett went home ages ago. I know you're a
busy man, but I think—no, I'm sure—that you're
avoiding me. Finn saw you this morning, and he said
you were on top of the world. Has something happened while you were away?'

She paused to study his quiet face. It took a bit of
an effort to go on, and it would sound silly and child-
ish, but it had to be said. 'Did you meet someone—

a woman—and fall in love with her? Because if you did you don't need to worry about telling me. I'll understand, I promise you, and it would make me very happy for you.'

She sat back. 'There, I've said it. Sometimes one simply has to say exactly what one thinks. I can say it to you because we're friends.'

He said quietly, 'Why would it make you happy, Francesca?'

'Well, I don't really want to answer that question, but it might explain why I've said all this. You see, I love you, and I want you to be happy more than anything else in the world.'

The professor found himself smiling. He got up, went round his desk and pulled Franny gently to her feet, her hands in his.

'Shall I tell you why I was on top of the world? It was because I was coming home to you, my darling. Falling in love with you was something I had no intention of doing, and I fought hard against it. I thought that I had everything in life that I needed, and then you came into it and into my heart.'

Franny mumbled, 'Then why didn't you say so…?'

The professor put his arms around her. 'Perhaps I am too old for you, too set in my ways. That you should love me seemed such a remote possibility that I was afraid to see you again, even though I longed to. I knew when I came home that I would have to tell you that I loved you. I was sitting here wondering how to do it.'

'I'll tell you how to do it,' said Franny. 'I think it might be something which gets easier as you go along, as it were.'

'My dearest little love, what an adorable creature you are...' He bent and kissed her, taking his time about it.

'That was very nice,' said Franny, and was kissed again. For someone too old for her and set in his ways, he kissed in a most satisfactory fashion. She couldn't resist asking him, 'You're sure that you love me? I'm not beautiful or clever, and I talk too much.'

He put a hand under her chin and looked down at her with tenderness. 'You are beautiful and clever and kind, and the day you stop talking I shall die, my darling.'

It was a reply to satisfy the most doubtful of girls. Franny reached up and put her arms round his neck. 'We are going to be very happy—you won't mind if our little girls talk as much as I do?'

'I shall find it delightful, provided we even things up with a boy or two.'

'Two of each,' said Franny, 'then they can make up a tennis four.'

The professor gave a great shout of laughter. 'At least you don't hanker after a cricket eleven.' He hugged the breath from her body and kissed her, a gentle kiss, setting the seal on their happiness.

MILLS & BOON®

Makes any time special™

Mills & Boon publish 29 new titles every month. Select from...

Modern Romance™ **Tender Romance™**

Sensual Romance™

Medical Romance™ **Historical Romance™**

MAT2